Advanced Introduction to Law and Religion

Elgar Advanced Introductions are stimulating and thoughtful introductions to major fields in the social sciences, business and law, expertly written by the world's leading scholars. Designed to be accessible yet rigorous, they offer concise and lucid surveys of the substantive and policy issues associated with discrete subject areas.

The aims of the series are two-fold: to pinpoint essential principles of a particular field, and to offer insights that stimulate critical thinking. By distilling the vast and often technical corpus of information on the subject into a concise and meaningful form, the books serve as accessible introductions for undergraduate and graduate students coming to the subject for the first time. Importantly, they also develop well-informed, nuanced critiques of the field that will challenge and extend the understanding of advanced students, scholars and policy-makers.

For a full list of titles in the series please see the back of the book. Recent titles in the series include:

Disaster Risk Reduction
Douglas Paton

Social Movements and Political Protests
Karl-Dieter Opp

Radical Innovation
Joe Tidd

Pricing Strategy and Analytics
Vithala R. Rao

Bounded Rationality
Clement A. Tisdell

International Food Law
Neal D. Fortin

International Conflict and Security Law, Second Edition
Nigel D. White

Entrepreneurial Finance, Second Edition
Hans Landström

US Civil Liberties
Susan N. Herman

Resilience
Fikret Berkes

Insurance Law
Robert H. Jerry, III

Law and Religion
Frank S. Ravitch

Advanced Introduction to

Law and Religion

FRANK S. RAVITCH

Professor of Law and Walter H. Stowers Chair of Law and Religion, Director Kyoto Japan Program, Michigan State University College of Law, USA

Elgar Advanced Introductions

Cheltenham, UK • Northampton, MA, USA

© Frank S. Ravitch 2023

All rights reserved. No part of this publication may be reproduced, stored in a retrieval system or transmitted in any form or by any means, electronic, mechanical or photocopying, recording, or otherwise without the prior permission of the publisher.

Published by
Edward Elgar Publishing Limited
The Lypiatts
15 Lansdown Road
Cheltenham
Glos GL50 2JA
UK

Edward Elgar Publishing, Inc.
William Pratt House
9 Dewey Court
Northampton
Massachusetts 01060
USA

A catalogue record for this book
is available from the British Library

Library of Congress Control Number: 2023931534

This book is available electronically on *Elgar Advanced Introductions: Law*
www.advancedintros.com

Printed on elemental chlorine free (ECF)
recycled paper containing 30% Post-Consumer Waste

ISBN 978 1 78990 404 8 (cased)
ISBN 978 1 78990 406 2 (paperback)
ISBN 978 1 78990 405 5 (eBook)

Printed and bound in the USA

This book is dedicated to my daughters Elysha and Ariana; my wife Chika; and my parents Arline and Carl, who are an inspiration and amazing examples of the best humanity can be.

Contents

Acknowledgements		ix
	Introduction to *Law and Religion*	**1**
1	**Basic concepts**	**3**
	1.1 The sources of law governing law and religion issues and religious institutions	3
	1.2 Conceptual foundations	4
2	**Religious freedom**	**24**
	2.1 Introduction	24
	2.2 Who is protected	24
	2.3 Exemptions from general laws	27
	2.4 Rights versus rights: when religious freedom claims conflict with the rights of others	39
	2.5 Discrimination against religion	45
	2.6 Discrimination by religion	51
3	**Government support for religion: public education**	**54**
	3.1 Introduction	54
	3.2 Public schools	55
4	**Government support for religion: public property**	**78**
	4.1 Public property	78
	4.2 Free speech and the public/private distinction	99
	4.3 Legislative prayer	103
	4.4 Ceremonial deism	105

viii   ADVANCED INTRODUCTION TO LAW AND RELIGION

5   Government support for religion: funding and tax exemptions   **106**
5.1   Funding   106
5.2   Tax exemptions and related benefits   111

6   Religious autonomy   **124**
6.1   Introduction   124
6.2   Intrareligious disputes   124
6.3   Hiring, supervision, and retention of clergy and others   135
6.4   Liability of religious entities for employee conduct, including clergy abuse   139

7   Conclusion   **145**

Index   147

Acknowledgements

There are many people whom I would like to thank for their support and advice during the writing and production of this book: my wife Chika and my daughters Elysha and Ariana, whose brilliance, thoughtfulness, and love make life brighter and add balance to everything I do; my parents, Carl and Arline Ravitch, who are a source of constant support and love, and who are an inspiration for all three of their children; my late Bubby and Pop Pop, who are always close to my heart, and who embodied all that is best in religion and in law, without being lawyers or overtly religious; my sisters Sharon and Elizabeth and their families; my Uncle Gary and Aunt Mindy and my Aunt Jackie and Uncle Ken, who have been exceptionally supportive of all my work, and who each in their own way have an interest in law and/or religion.

I am grateful to the Michigan State University College of Law, which supported some of my work on this book with a summer research grant, and to Jane Meland, Hildur Hannah, and the staff of the Michigan State University College of Law Library for their help and support, as well as Dean Linda Greene who has been exceptionally supportive of faculty research and publications. I am also grateful to Stephen Harries, Fiona Todd, Kirsty Barker, and Katherine King at Edward Elgar Publishing for inviting me to write this book and bringing it to fruition.

Introduction to *Law and Religion*

Law and religion is a vast field covering the many issues that arise when government and religion come into contact, as well as a number of issues entirely in the private sphere. The field of law and religion also includes religious law, for example canon law, halacha, and sharia. While religious law is a fascinating topic—one worthy of many volumes—it is beyond the scope of this book.

This book will focus on the relationship between government and religion, including religious freedom, the level of separation between government and religion, and the role of courts in deciding religious questions. It will also address some situations in the private sphere, such as the ways in which law may govern discrimination by private entities based on religion or based on religious concerns.

The focus of the book will be global, but two sorts of system are not addressed in this book. The first is the theocracy, such as Saudi Arabia and Iran. These systems raise a wide range of important law and religion questions, but they are quite different from the systems in the majority of countries around the world. Therefore, theocratic systems cannot be adequately addressed in this book, which focuses primarily on law and religion in democratic, or similar, systems.

The second is the authoritarian regime, such as North Korea, Turkmenistan, and to some extent China, where government control over religion is almost complete. Of course, a number of countries have systems that share some traits with theocracies and/or authoritarian regimes but do not completely fit the description. Examples include Myanmar and Russia, which are engaged in systematic persecution of the Rohingya and Jehovah's Witnesses, respectively. Those studying law and religion in these systems may find this book helpful to the extent that the systems share a few limited traits with more democratic systems.

The book is structured around categories often seen in US law because many other systems use the same or similar categories. The analysis of some of the topics within each category, however, will go beyond US law. Moreover, this book assumes the reader is familiar with major issues in law and religion as well as some of the theoretical debates surrounding those issues. Thus, this book is not a basic introduction, but rather a more advanced primer on law and religion.

Significantly, this book is not, and cannot be, comprehensive, given the vast array of issues and approaches to those issues within law and religion. This book will use examples from certain countries or systems to illustrate the main approaches to each issue, but it will not explore every approach or every legal system. So, for example, on the question of religious exceptions to general laws the book will explore the approaches used in the US and Japan and by the European Commission on Human Rights (ECHR), as these systems have similarities and differences that allow for exploration of the main approaches used in many systems throughout the world. Throughout the book the US will remain a primary focus because litigation (and to a lesser extent legislation) impacting law and religion is more pervasive in the US than perhaps in any other democratic system.

1 Basic concepts

1.1 The sources of law governing law and religion issues and religious institutions

Before exploring the substantive law and theoretical concepts governing the interactions between government and religion, it is useful to briefly touch on the array of legal sources which govern these questions. These sources include constitutions, legislation, regulations, treaties, common law, and international law. Not all systems use all these sources, and the importance of the sources may vary from system to system.

For example, in the United States the US Constitution and state constitutions play an important role in governing the legality of interactions between government and religion. Yet, legislation also plays an important role through statutes such as the Federal Religious Freedom Restoration Act (RFRA) and §501(C)(3) of the United States Tax Code, as well as state Religious Freedom Restoration Acts and state tax laws. Moreover, regulations put in place by agencies such as the Equal Employment Opportunity Commission can be important in the employment discrimination context and Internal Revenue Service regulations can be important in the tax context.

In the European Union, national laws, including constitutions, legislation, and regulations, often govern initial decisions about interactions between government and religion. These decisions can however be appealed to the European Court of Justice (ECJ) when conflict with EU law is alleged. Moreover, cases can go to the European Court of Human Rights (ECHR), which has jurisdiction to interpret the European Convention on Human Rights when a nation is alleged to have violated that Convention. The

4 ADVANCED INTRODUCTION TO LAW AND RELIGION

relationship between the ECJ and the ECHR is complex and will be addressed a bit in later chapters.

In Japan, Articles 20 and 89 of the Constitution govern questions involving the interaction between religion and government, but there is also national legislation such as the Religious Juridical Persons Act (宗教法人法 *Shuukyou Houjin Hou*) that governs rights and benefits for religious entities that choose to register under the Act. Moreover, prefectural and local laws may also govern issues such as religious discrimination or land use by religious entities.

These are just a few of the many examples that exist in the law and religion context. Key is that a number of sources may govern law and religion questions and therefore those with an interest in a specific country or jurisdiction should familiarize themselves with the variety of legal sources that govern law and religion questions in that jurisdiction. Importantly, looking just to the United States Constitution to answer religious freedom questions in the US would be vastly deficient given the important role that RFRAs and/or state constitutions can play in these situations. Similarly, looking at only national law when considering religious freedom questions in an EU member state may miss the role of the ECJ and the Maastricht Treaty and/or the role of the ECHR and the European Convention on Human Rights.

This book will be organized around the types of questions that arise in law and religion and not around the sources of law that govern those questions. Still, this section should serve as a reference for the general legal sources that govern law and religion questions.

1.2 Conceptual foundations

A wide range of conceptual foundations have been influential in the law and religion context. Some of the more common and important conceptual foundations are the principles of equality, liberty, neutrality, separation, accommodation, tradition, and nonpreferentialism. These principles work alone or together in a variety of contexts. There is often disagreement among scholars as to which principles should govern generally or in specific situations. Some principles, such as separationism

BASIC CONCEPTS   5

and nonpreferentialism, are more likely to come into play in situations involving government support for religion. Others, such as equality and liberty, may arise in a wide array of law and religion situations.

Neutrality has been viewed as a central principle for law and religion cases in many systems, including those of the US and Japan and the European Convention on Human Rights. Yet, as will be seen, neutrality raises some unique problems both practically and conceptually; problems with which courts and scholars have regularly grappled.

1.2.1 Equality

The principle of equality is central in many systems and has been a particular focus of scholarly and judicial discussion in the US. But what is this principle, and how does it function in the law and religion context? These may seem like simple questions; however, the answers are anything but.

At the broadest level there seems to be agreement that government should not be able to discriminate against religious individuals or groups, but what counts as discrimination and how far this principle goes are the subject of significant debate. The recent COVID-19 restriction exemption cases in the US provide a striking example of how far the discrimination concept might be stretched and how disagreement over what counts as discrimination can impact outcomes.[1]

Consider the following questions. Is it discrimination against religion to treat churches the same as theaters and gyms regarding restrictions during a pandemic? Is it discrimination to treat churches differently than grocery stores regarding restrictions during a pandemic? The United States Supreme Court initially held that states should have broad leeway during a pandemic to restrict gatherings where people may stay inside

---

[1] For example, compare *Roman Catholic Diocese of Brooklyn v Cuomo*, 529 U.S. ___, 141 S.Ct. 63, 208 L.Ed.2d 206 (2020) (granting injunctive relief against a New York order creating occupancy limits of 10 or 25 people in areas hard hit by COVID-19, and holding that because secular businesses, including grocery stores, were not subject to the same limits, the limits on churches and other houses of worship was discriminatory) with *South Bay United Pentecostal Church v Newsom*, 590 U.S. ___, 140 S.Ct. 1613, 207 L.Ed.2d 154 (2020) (denying injunctive relief to a church that challenged an order limiting attendance at indoor events).

6 ADVANCED INTRODUCTION TO LAW AND RELIGION

a single location for a long period of time and/or sing.[2] This would suggest that churches are more similar to theaters and restaurants than to grocery stores. Yet, less than five months later the Court held that New York could not restrict church attendance so long as grocery stores and retail shops could remain open.[3]

In this context the comparison group is key to determining whether there is discrimination. Is a church, synagogue, or mosque more like a theater or a grocery store? Despite compelling evidence supporting the state's assertions that religious services are more like theaters or restaurants, with singing and longer attendance in one place, the US Supreme Court sided with the religious entities. Thus, while all the Justices agree that discrimination against religion is problematic, the delineation of comparison entities can predetermine the outcome of any discrimination analysis.

A simpler scenario would be where government is clearly disfavoring a specific religion(s) or favoring a specific religion(s) to the detriment of others, but even then, things are not always so simple. For example, the US Supreme Court recently upheld legislative prayer offered primarily by Christian ministers and priests at town council meetings where members of the council regularly crossed themselves and participated in the prayer, often before hearing citizen requests for action or remedies from the town council.[4] There was also evidence in the record suggesting that at the very least there was structural favoritism toward Christian prayer givers, and even some evidence of overt discrimination against those who opposed the prayer.[5]

As a matter of US law, the difference between upholding the prayer in this case and striking down the New York State COVID-19 restrictions mentioned above may be justified by the fact that the prayer case was brought under the Establishment Clause of the United States Constitution and the COVID-19 exemption case under the Free Exercise Clause of the United States Constitution. Yet, this does not make the results any less

---

[2] *South Bay United Pentecostal Church v Newsom*, 590 U.S. ___, 140 S.Ct. 1613, 207 L.Ed.2d 154 (2020).

[3] *Roman Catholic Diocese of Brooklyn v Cuomo*, 529 U.S. ___, 141 S.Ct. 63, 208 L.Ed.2d 206 (2020).

[4] *Town of Greece v Galloway*, 572 U.S. 565 (2014).

[5] *Id.* (Justice Kagan dissenting).

problematic under the principle of equality, especially given the evidence of at least some overt discrimination in the prayer case (something that was lacking in the COVID-19 restriction case)[6] and the fact that in both cases the decisions and conduct of government actors were considered by the Court and given vastly different deference.

In other words, even if one can legally justify the difference in results, that difference does not seem to serve the principle of equality well. Similar results arise when considering French *laïcité* and the treatment of Jewish and Muslim headwear versus Christian crosses. A 2004 law passed in France banned students from wearing conspicuous religious attire such as yarmulkas, hijabs, and large crosses.[7] Two factors render this law discriminatory. First is the obvious fact, well understood at the time, that the primary target of the law was the hijab and to some extent the yarmulka. Second is the fact that, even without such targeting, the reality is that under both Halacha and Sharia, the size of a yarmulka or a hijab has inner limits below which they cannot serve their religious function, and obviously neither can be worn inside the head. Yet a cross could be tucked under a shirt and for the most part a smaller cross may serve a similar function to a large one. Yet, the argument was that the law promoted the principal of *laïcité*, which itself is argued to promote equality. Of course, as in the US cases mentioned above, the system was structured in a manner that favors the dominant religion or a secularized tolerance of it. Moreover, the results, while perhaps legally justifiable in the relevant systems, still discriminate and violate the principal of equality if understood to require anything more than formal equality.

Thus, even when confronting questions involving discrimination against religion or a specific religion(s), the parameters of the equality principle are not always clear, except in the easiest cases. The examples from the US and France suggest that there is no Archimedean point from outside a given system's cultural or structural biases from which equality is likely to be interpreted. This does not prevent decision-making from occurring; nor does it mean that equality is never possible. It does mean, however, that the ideal of equality is best met when decision makers are able to reflect on the systemic biases that may be influencing their analysis.

---

[6]   *Id.*

[7]   Law No. 2004-228 of Mar. 15, 2004, Journal Officiel de la République Française [J.O.] [Official Gazette of France], Mar. 17, 2004, 5190.

Considering these biases may not change the outcome given other legal principles, but it may lead to more open engagement with the principle of equality and the other principles mentioned below.

Beyond cases involving discrimination, many questions can arise under the principle of equality. Examples include questions such as: Who can access government funding or tax breaks? What should happen when a law has a disparate impact on certain religions even if there is no other evidence of discrimination? What happens when government favors religion, or a specific religion?

There are a variety of answers to these questions within individual legal systems, but the principle of equality would suggest that at the very least, specific religion(s) should not be given preferential treatment regarding government funding or tax breaks over other religions or nonreligious entities. Of course, this raises complex questions about what counts as preferential treatment, a topic about which scholars have written numerous volumes without coming to a general consensus and to which legal systems have given a variety of answers. Tax breaks and funding will be addressed in detail in Chapter 5.

The disparate impact question arises most obviously in the context of religious exemptions to generally applicable laws discussed in depth in section 2.3. At a conceptual level, there are two competing equality arguments at play in exemption cases. First is the argument that denying exemptions naturally favors more dominant religions or secularity in a given society, and frequently disadvantages religious minorities, whose practices are often poorly understood or not considered by legislatures and other decisionmakers. Second is the argument that any system of exemptions for religion favors religion over nonreligious ethical, philosophical, or other systems of belief or commitment, thus privileging religion.

These two concepts are not inherently in conflict because technically denying all religious exemptions or granting all exemptions whether religious or not (often balanced against the government interests in not granting exemptions) would arguably prevent a disparate impact. Yet, the practical reality is that the burden of a system which undervalues religious exemptions is most likely to fall on religious minorities, because laws tend to reflect the needs of larger and/or more powerful groups within

BASIC CONCEPTS 9

society. Of course, a similar burden may also fall on other, less common nonreligious belief systems, but under the principle of equality this would arguably militate in favor of granting both sorts of exemptions, balanced against social interests, rather than denying both sorts of exemptions.

Finally, the principle of equality can be implicated when government favors, or appears to favor, religion or specific religions. This is especially true when the favored religion(s) is more dominant in society. There are a wide array of situations where this sort of favoritism appears and the literature on these situations fills hundreds of thousands of pages. Much of this literature explicitly or implicitly raises equality questions. These situations will be addressed in depth in Chapter 3.

The equality principle suggests that at the very least, government should not favor or disfavor a particular religion or religion generally. Yet, this sort of favoring or disfavoring has happened in almost every legal system. Sometimes dominant religions or more established religions are explicitly favored; sometimes certain religions generally appear endorsed or supported by government in ways that other belief systems are not; sometimes smaller or less established religions are disfavored; and sometimes the dominant religion(s) is viewed as just a cultural phenomenon when given explicit or implicit government support or largesse, while other religions are not. In many situations the very question of what counts as favoring or disfavoring is itself the central issue.

An in-depth discussion of the equality principle is beyond the scope of this advanced introduction. This brief discussion should, however, provide an outline of some of the major questions that arise with the principle of equality. The specific situations in which equality and the other principles discussed herein have been operating in the background are the focus of Chapters 2–4.

1.2.2 Liberty

Religious liberty is a powerful idea, and one that a number of systems attempt to safeguard. This, however, raises the question: What *is* religious liberty? Several schools of thought have arisen in this context, but their concepts of religious liberty are sometimes in conflict and often produce conflicting results. There is no Archimedean point from outside a given approach that can claim to demonstrate "the" meaning of religious liberty. Religious liberty either must be tied to some baseline or may be best viewed as an aspiration to be fulfilled by whatever approach may best support it in a given system.

For example, consider Free Exercise Clause exemptions. The reasoning is by now standard (and I would argue valid). That is, laws of "general applicability" sometimes interfere with religious practice, and, in fact, are more likely to interfere with the religious practices of those who are not in the religious mainstream. This is attenuated by the fact that the dominant religion in the United States and many other countries is heavily faith-based (although that is a highly oversimplified description), and that many minority religions are practice-oriented. These practices are not mere preferences in most contexts, but rather are central to the faiths of the practitioners. Thus, laws of general applicability should not be allowed to interfere with these practices without a compelling governmental interest and narrow tailoring. To find otherwise is to interfere with a central aspect of religious liberty.

Yet there is an easy response that also claims to be consistent with religious liberty: that faith and belief are absolutely protected, but practice must conform to the public good. Therefore, laws of general applicability do not require religious exemptions, even though this might be helpful to some religious practitioners. Everyone has the same level of protection for religious liberty, but unfortunately some religions or religious practices will be more impacted by laws of general applicability than others, and there is no absolute right to religious liberty that bests the interest in maintaining social order. Each of the above approaches could claim that it is consistent with the principle of religious liberty.

Just from this example we can see two of the competing theories of religious liberty. First, that religious liberty cannot be complete unless we protect both belief and practice to the greatest extent possible, and this sometimes requires exceptions to general laws unless the government's interest in not providing an exemption is significant or compelling. This means religious practices can conflict with what is perceived as the public good, but not to an extent that significantly interferes with the public good. Second, that religious liberty inheres in protecting religious faith and conscience but does not extend to protecting religious practices, or at least those that conflict with what is perceived as the public good.

BASIC CONCEPTS   11

Another approach views religious freedom as the single most important freedom and would allow religious liberty to overpower, and even harm, competing rights. On the other end of the spectrum is an approach that views religious liberty as just one in a panoply of rights and freedoms, and no more important than the others. There are a range of views within each of these approaches, both theoretically and based on context.

Therefore, some theorists argue that individual religious liberty, and that of religious entities, is more important than other forms of liberty. Others argue that religious liberty is just a small part of the broader panoply of conscience claims and no more worthy of protection than the others. Moreover, in some systems religious liberty may be available only to certain religions but not others, and in other systems religious liberty is available to anyone with a sincerely held religious belief.

At its broadest, religious liberty is more a platitude than a principle. When we try to define it, we are faced with competing and contestable notions of what religious liberty is, and thus the concept cannot rely on a provable baseline of "true liberty," but rather must rely on other concepts or doctrinal tests to fill the gap. The legal concept of religious liberty may operate best through accommodation (discussed below), but even there, competing views of religious liberty preclude one baseline of religious liberty from being "the" correct view.

1.2.3   Neutrality

Steven Smith has explained:

> [T]he quest for neutrality, despite its understandable appeal and the tenacity with which it has been pursued, is an attempt to grasp at an illusion. Upon reflection, this failure should not be surprising. The impossibility of a truly "neutral" theory of religious freedom is analogous to the impossibility, recognized by modern philosophers, of finding some outside Archimedean point [...] from which to look down on and describe reality. Descriptions of reality are always undertaken from a point within reality. In the same way, theories of religious freedom are always offered from the viewpoint of one of the competing positions that generate the need for such a theory; there is no neutral vantage point that can permit the theorist or judge to transcend these competing positions. Hence, insofar as a genuine and satisfactory theory of religious freedom would need to be "neutral" in this sense, rather than one that

12 ADVANCED INTRODUCTION TO LAW AND RELIGION

privileges one of the competing positions from the outset, a theory of religious freedom is as illusory as the ideal of neutrality it seeks to embody.[8]

Many other scholars have acknowledged the elusive and malleable nature of neutrality.[9] Therefore, answers to the question "What is neutrality?" have been at best variable and elusive at an epistemological level. At a practical level, neutrality has meant different things even within the same system. For example, in the US, the US Supreme Court originally used the concept of separationism as the hallmark of neutrality in the Establishment Clause context. Currently, the Court often uses formal neutrality, which is significantly at odds with separationism. In between, the Court used various versions of neutrality, including what Douglas Laycock has called "substantive neutrality," which views neutrality as minimizing government encouragement or discouragement of religion.[10]

Similarly, in the free exercise context the US Supreme Court has used various approaches to neutrality, including both the view that mandating exemptions to generally applicable laws is neutral and the directly opposite view. More recently, the Court has expanded the concept of neutrality in the context of what counts as discrimination under the Free Exercise Clause. All of this is discussed further in Chapter 2.

Neutrality has also been an important concept in the ECHR. Since at least 2000, the ECHR has held that states have a duty to remain neutral in matters of religion. Yet the ECHR, like the US Supreme Court, has been all over the board on what counts as religious neutrality, sometimes seemingly allowing serious redefinitions and/or violations of the principle by national governments.

Given the malleability of the concept of neutrality, none of this should be surprising. Neutrality is broad and vague enough to be used to support a variety of perspectives, including perspectives in direct conflict with each other. Neutrality is nothing more than a variable social construction.

---

[8]   STEVEN D. SMITH, FOREORDAINED FAILURE: THE QUEST FOR A CONSTITUTIONAL PRINCIPLE OF RELIGIOUS FREEDOM 96-97 (Oxford Univ. Press 1999).

[9]   See e.g., FRANK S. RAVITCH, MASTERS OF ILLUSION: THE SUPREME COURT AND THE RELIGION CLAUSES (NYU Press 2007).

[10] Douglas Laycock, Formal, Substantive, and Disaggregated Neutrality Toward Religion, 39 DEPAUL L. REV. 993 (1990).

BASIC CONCEPTS   13

Yet this social construction can take on practical meaning when tied to a particular baseline.[11] Of course, the baseline does all the work and there is no Archimedean point from outside a baseline or system from which the baseline can be proven neutral.

Issues surrounding governmental interaction with religion have become increasingly complex over the past hundred years or so as governments have grown and gotten involved in many areas of life where there was traditionally little or no government participation or regulation. It is hard for government to act "neutrally" when its actions or failure to act in the same situation can have massive repercussions. This creates problems for any "neutrality" test that must be applied to this massive web of government action and inaction. At the theoretical level, such a test cannot make an absolute claim to neutrality, because there is no principle of super-neutrality to demonstrate a tests' neutrality; contested perspectives necessarily enter the process of developing such a test. It would solve the problem if one could prove neutrality by looking at the impact of a court's approach, but this is impossible to do without presuming that a certain baseline is neutral and using the presumed baseline to justify the neutrality of outcomes. Therefore, when this book uses the term neutrality in later sections and chapters it should be understood that this is not support for any epistemic claim to neutrality, but rather referring to a particular baseline that is referred to as "neutral" or "neutrality" in a given system.

Therefore, terms such as formal neutrality, neutrality of results, state neutrality, substantive neutrality, and separation as neutrality will be used in various contexts later in this book. If the term "neutrality" is used by itself, it will either be in the context of one of these baselines or in discussing specific legislation or decisions by courts or the ECHR.

1.2.4   Separationism

Separation between church and state (or separationism) is an approach that has been used in several systems. Two well-known examples are early Establishment Clause cases in the US and the concept of "*seiji to shuukyou no bunri*" (政治と宗教の分離), "separation of politics and religion" in Japan. The US Supreme Court has moved away from separationism in

---

[11]   *See e.g.*, ANDREW KOPPELMAN, DEFENDING AMERICAN RELIGIOUS NEUTRALITY (Harvard Univ. Press 2013).

14   ADVANCED INTRODUCTION TO LAW AND RELIGION

many contexts over the past 25 years or so. Japan has been truer to the ideal of separationism in recent years than the US, but there are exceptions there too.

In the US the historical arguments for and against separationism are both supported by a variety of sources. There are many variables at play in gleaning the intent, understandings, and practices of the many framers and state ratifying conventions in the US. If, however, we look to the broad intent of the framers and interpret historical practices and principles in light of today's diverse society and massive government, the argument for separation may be stronger. This section does not attempt to take sides in this historical debate. As a result, separation can be a broad or limited concept depending on how we define it. There can be degrees of separation.

This can be seen in Japan, where some practices that are connected to traditional Shinto have been allowed at government events because they are viewed more as culture than religion, while other practices such as financial support and government offerings or other support for shrines are considered unconstitutional. From a Western perspective some of these cases and situations might seem confusing, and this author has written a lot about the bases and reasons for this confusion. For present purposes, however, it is enough to note that the perception of religion and the role of organized religion in Japan are quite different from the West.

In both the US and Japan, many scholars and courts have long recognized that "strict separation" is impossible, because at least at the margins there is bound to be some interaction between religion and government. Strict separation would amount to establishing a purely secular state, where secularism is at least implicitly encouraged and favored, and religion banished from the public square and public life. Moreover, it would be impossible—or at the very least highly impractical—to maintain strict separation, given the many areas in which religion and government might incidentally touch upon each other.

Even in systems with conceptually strong separation, like the French concept of *laïcité*, strict separation is not maintained because the state still supports religious schools and as a practical matter may favor dominant religious symbols over others in the public sphere. Of course, Europe has a diverse group of systems in the context of religion–state relations.

France has one of the stronger concepts of separation and promotion of secularism, but French separation is not strict in the absolute sense of that term, given the funding that goes to schools and to maintain historical sites such as cathedrals.

Another way to apply separation is to use a contextual approach, such as prohibiting government-endorsed religious exercises or direct aid to religious institutions as a limit on separationism. Thus, separation would be defined by a context and a test, not by a broad notion of absolute separation. Relatedly, it is possible to use separation as a guiding baseline in some contexts, but not others. Thus, for example, separation might be used as a baseline in the school prayer context, the public school-curriculum context, and perhaps the direct aid context in the US, but not in equal access or indirect aid cases. This is not too far from the current situation in the US. The current situation in the US, though, is more a result of the positions of the swing voters on the Court, few of whom take a consistent separationist position, than of a dedication to separation on these issues. Additionally, two decisions by the US Supreme Court in 2022 may throw the entire enterprise of separation in the US into question. These decisions will be discussed further in Chapters 2 and 3.

In France separation might guide decisions on public displays of religion and private religious expression in public spaces, but not in the context of school funding. This seems to be close to the current situation there as well.

Depending on which baseline one picks for separationism, it could function as a narrow test, a broad principle that urges as much separation between the government and religion as possible, or something in between. Therefore, separation can operate at a practical level because nations can choose if, where, and how to implement it. The key is that some degree of separation is possible and has been implemented in a variety of systems.

1.2.5 Accommodation

Like separation, accommodation can arguably function both at the level of a broad principle and as a narrow principle, or as a facet of a doctrinal test. Accommodationist arguments are most common under the Free Exercise Clause in the US and can also be seen in exemption situations in

16 ADVANCED INTRODUCTION TO LAW AND RELIGION

Europe and Japan. In the US, accommodation supports exemptions from laws of general applicability. Accommodation can also be used to support concepts of religious autonomy for religious entities.

The question of religious exemptions will be addressed in detail in Chapter 2 and the doctrine of religious autonomy for religious entities will be addressed in detail in Chapter 4. For present purposes it is important to understand that accommodation is what it sounds like, namely, an approach that focuses on providing accommodations to enable religious practice and religious thriving. In some approaches to accommodation this means potentially favoring religion while in others it means simply allowing exemptions where general laws interfere with religious practice in a significant way and an exemption can be given without significantly harming the public good.

In the US, accommodationist arguments are often seen in the free exercise context and support providing exemptions to generally applicable laws. Statutes such as RFRA promote an accommodationist approach. Similar concepts exist under the ECHR (although rulings have been inconsistent), under Article 20 of the Japanese Constitution, and in South Africa. As will be explained in Chapter 2, in all of these systems, except the US in recent years, religious accommodations cannot interfere with the rights of others.

In some systems, accommodation may be argued to allow government support for religion. Social conservatives and others in the US have famously argued for government promotion of religion and/or Christianity specifically. This would go beyond what most scholars refer to as accommodation, but social conservatives argue that recognizing Christian traditions is simply to accommodate the heritage and traditions of the US. These are weak arguments for a variety of practical and historical reasons, but in recent years the US Supreme Court has moved closer to this perspective without embracing all of its broader implications. In Europe, several national systems are structured based on the assumption that aid to religion simply accommodates the needs of citizens and/or religious entities, but of course in most of these systems there is no constitutional prohibition on government promotion of religion.

1.2.6 Nonpreferentialism

Nonpreferentialism is the idea that government can favor religion over irreligion but cannot favor one religion over another. This approach has been advocated by former US Supreme Court Justice Rehnquist and a few other Justices over the years but has never commanded a majority of the Court, although recent developments in the makeup of the US Supreme Court may change this. It has also been advocated by several prominent scholars in the US and elsewhere, but it is not the favored approach among most scholars.

Nonpreferentialism is a concept best known in the US, but there are some other systems around the world where in limited contexts religion can be favored over irreligion—especially in regard to government aid to religion—but one religion cannot be favored over others. For example, there are hints of nonpreferentialism in the private school funding systems in both Germany and France, where a variety of religious schools can receive funding. Yet neither the French nor the German systems as a whole are nonreferential. In Germany there are ways in which dominant religions get far more benefits than less dominant religions in terms of church taxes and other legal structures, and also areas where secularism can be favored over religion. In France, it is specifically acceptable for government to favor secularism over religion in public life. Thus, as a holistic concept for church–state relations, nonpreferentialism has mostly been an issue in the US, although it has never commanded a majority of the US Supreme Court or the majority of law and religion scholars.

1.2.7 Tradition

Many systems look to social, political, and cultural traditions, including those that have religious elements, when deciding questions about the appropriate relationship between government and religion and/or questions about separation of religion and the state (in systems that use that concept). Yet, in the United States, "tradition" has taken on the mantle of a legal test in some cases under the Establishment Clause. This has been especially true in cases involving religious displays on public property and in cases involving legislative prayer.

The legislative prayer cases reflect a theme: Because the First Congress which drafted and ratified the First Amendment had legislative prayer, legislative prayer does not violate the First Amendment. Over the years

18 ADVANCED INTRODUCTION TO LAW AND RELIGION

there has been debate over the propriety of this rule and whether there are exceptions to it. For example, from the first legislative prayer case, decided in 1983, until 2014 it was generally understood that legislative prayer had to be nonsectarian and non-proselytizing to be constitutional under the "tradition" approach.[12]

The general "tradition" concept has been applied in some other situations, such as religious symbolism on public land. In a series of cases involving longstanding monuments the Court has used a sort of tradition test to analyze those monuments, most recently in 2019.[13] These cases will be explored further in Chapter 3. Moreover, there have been concurring and dissenting opinions in a variety of cases arguing for an expansion of, or for the abandonment of, the "tradition" approach. Finally, in two shocking cases decided in 2022, and discussed in more detail in Chapters 2 and 3, the Court expanded the tradition approach so that it may now be the main approach to Establishment Clause issues in the US.

1.2.8   What is religion?

One of the most vexing questions facing courts and legal systems around the world is what counts as "religion" for legal purposes. This question has vexed philosophers, religion scholars, anthropologists, sociologists, legal scholars, and legal practitioners for many years (many centuries, in the case of philosophers and religion scholars). There is no easy answer to this question because the demarcation point between religion and general philosophical or moral codes is not clear and preconceptions about religion may influence what a given system counts as religion.

Libraries-worth of material has been written on this topic and the broader debates are beyond the scope of this book. Given the focus of this book as an advanced introduction to law and religion, this section will focus on what several legal systems have done (or not done) in trying to define religion. Nothing in this book should be read as asserting that any of these definitions are adequate, or that it is even possible to create a metaphys-

---

[12] Compare *Marsh v Chambers*, 463 U.S. 783 (1983) and *Wynne v Town of Great Falls*, 376 F.3d 292 (U.S. Court of Appeals, 4th Cir. 2004), with *Town of Greece v Galloway*, 572 U.S. 565 (2014).

[13] *American Legion v American Humanist Association*, ___ U.S. ___, 139 S.Ct. 2067, 204 L.Ed.2d 452 (2019).

BASIC CONCEPTS   19

ically coherent demarcation point between religion and other strongly held belief systems.

In situations involving government support for religion, there is usually little question that the thing being supported would widely be considered religion. This is true in both the context of systems that prohibit government support for religion and those that allow it in given contexts. The US system provides many good examples of this in the Establishment Clause context, such as school prayer cases, cases involving funding for religious schools, and cases involving government support for religious symbols on government property. In these cases, the raison d'être for the lawsuit is that a government entity is supporting something that is commonly understood to be religious.

Even here, however, there are some challenging cases for courts and lawmakers around the world. For example, in a recent case from Japan, the Japanese Supreme Court addressed a land transaction where a local government in Okinawa gave land to a Confucianist Temple at no cost.[14] Whether Confucianism is a religion, a philosophy, or both is not widely agreed upon among scholars and even among some groups of Confucianists. In the case in question, however, the Japanese Supreme Court wisely avoided determining whether Confucianism in general is a religion and held that because this Confucianist Temple held various rituals, the temple counts as a religious place for purposes of Article 20 paragraph 3 of the Japanese Constitution, which has been interpreted to prohibit government aid, including grants of public property at no cost, to religious entities. Thus, the Court was able to address the question of whether the temple at issue in the case is religious in a functional manner, without addressing the broader question of whether Confucianism more generally is a religion.

Things get much harder when a definition of religion is needed to determine whether someone's freedom to live or practice their religion has been violated. Many of these situations involve faiths or practices that are generally agreed to be religion, but both the definition of religion and the vantage point from which it is made can have profound impacts.

---

[14]   Case seeking the revocation of the exemption from fixed asset tax, etc., 2019 (Gyo-Tsu) 222, Minshu Vol. 75, No. 2 (Judgment of 2/242021) (Grand Bench).

20   ADVANCED INTRODUCTION TO LAW AND RELIGION

Moreover, questions about whether cases involving someone with an individualized belief system, or one that is based in but deviates from the orthodoxy of a broader religion, should be protected by law arise in a number of situations.

Various legal systems around the world have grappled with these questions. Some have come to conclusions that limit what is recognized as religion based on their own cultural or socio-religious preconceptions. These systems tend to provide relatively bright-line definitions but are often criticized as being highly underinclusive and discriminatory against less well-established or uncommon groups. Other systems attempt to define religion very broadly to avoid having to create a clear definition for something that does not have a clear demarcation point. In this latter group the US system has served as an example, both good and bad, of how hard it can be to define religion in the religious freedom context.

In the US, the Supreme Court has addressed the question of what counts as religion on several occasions. From the perspective of a broad understanding of religion, the US Supreme Court's analysis of this issue got off to an inauspicious start. In *Davis v Beason*, the Court defined religion in terms far narrower than those of the modern Court:

> The term 'religion' has reference to one's views of his relations to his Creator, and to the obligations they impose of reverence for his being and character, and of obedience to his will. It is often confounded with the cultus or form of worship of a particular sect, but is distinguishable from the latter.[15]

More recent decisions have defined religion far more broadly than the *Davis* Court. For example, in *United States v Seeger*, a case involving three conscientious objectors to the Vietnam War, the Court provided the following definition: "The test might be stated in these words: a sincere and meaningful belief which occupies in the life of its possessor a place parallel to that filled by [] God."[16]

The *Seeger* case involved a provision of the Universal Military Training and Service Act, which the Court had to interpret to decide the case. The limited definition in that Act was challenged on First Amendment

---

[15]   133 U.S., 333, 342, 10 S.Ct. 299, 33 L.Ed. 637 (1890).
[16]   380 U.S. 163, 176, 85 S.Ct. 850, 13 L.Ed.2d 733 (1965).

grounds. In relation to the broad definition set forth above, the Court added that "the claim of the registrant that his belief is an essential part of a religious faith must be given great weight," but "while the 'truth' of a belief is not open to question, there remains the significant question whether it is 'truly held.'"[17]

In *Seeger*, all three of the objectors—Seeger, Jakobson, and Peter—met this test. Seeger stated "that his was a 'belief in and devotion to goodness and virtue for their own sakes, and a religious faith in a purely ethical creed.'" Jakobson stated that "he believed in a 'supreme being' who was the 'Creator of Man' in the sense of being 'ultimately responsible for the existence of' man and who was 'the Supreme Reality' of which 'the existence of man is the result.'" Peter stated that his beliefs could be called a belief in a supreme being, but that "[t]hese just do not happen to be the words I use." None of the three claimed to be members of any organized religion, although Seeger acknowledged agreement with a number of Quaker tenets. Yet all three claimed that their beliefs could be considered "religious" in the broad sense of that term.

How far the *Seeger* Court's definition of religion would extend when a claimant espouses a deeply held belief system that is not held out by the claimant to be "religious" remained an open question. The Court was clear, however, that the definition did not include those "whose beliefs are based on a 'merely personal moral code.'"

Five years after *Seeger*, the Court had the chance to answer the question about belief systems that a claimant does not hold out as religious. In *Welsh v United States*,[18] the Court held that a person was entitled to a conscientious objector exemption based on deep and sincere, but purely ethical and moral, beliefs, where those beliefs, though not religious, were held with the same strength as "more traditional religious convictions." Welsh had insisted that his beliefs were not religious beliefs, but the Court nonetheless held in his favor because "very few registrants are fully aware of the broad scope of the word 'religious'" as used in the relevant provision of the military law in question, "and accordingly a registrant's statement that his beliefs are nonreligious is a highly unreliable guide for those charged with administering the exemption." The Court acknowledged,

---

[17] *Id.* at 184–85.
[18] 398 U.S. 333, 90 S.Ct. 1792, 26 L.Ed.2d 308 (1970).

22   ADVANCED INTRODUCTION TO LAW AND RELIGION

as it had in *Seeger*, that a person's statement that his belief is religious is entitled to "great weight."

Relatedly, in *United States v Ballard*,[19] the Court held that it is not constitutional for government to put people "to the proof of their religious doctrines or beliefs." The Court continued: "Local boards and courts [...] are not free to reject beliefs because they consider them 'incomprehensible.' Their task is to decide whether the beliefs professed by a registrant are sincerely held and whether they are, in his own scheme of things, religious." Thus, government may not require anyone to prove the truth of his or her beliefs but may inquire whether the beliefs are sincerely held. Of course, government entities may make sure that the belief meets the Seeger–Welsh test—that is, that it is more than simply a personal moral belief which is not held with the same strength as more traditional religious convictions.

Seeger and *Welsh* were decided more than 50 years ago and involved conscientious objectors. Both cases are still good law in the US, but the Court has not directly revisited the issue since *Welsh* was decided in 1970, and it is unclear whether the current Court would define religion in the same way, or even whether it would consider it proper to attempt to define religion at all. Moreover, these cases specifically involved the question of conscientious objection to military service so whether these definitions are even workable in other contexts remains unclear.

The broad definition from these cases captures the difficulty of demarcating what religion is, and some have argued powerfully and persuasively that this makes protecting religious freedom a tenuous or even doomed enterprise.[20] The contrast between the early definition from the *Davis v Beason* case, which relied on a connection to a supreme being, and the later definitions from the *Welsh* and *Seeger* cases provides a microcosm of the difficulty in defining religion for legal purposes.

Definitions that try to be clear often rely on some connection to a supreme being, or specifically to G-d. These are often underinclusive of what may be considered as religion. Definitions that try to consider

---

[19]   322 U.S. 78, 64 S.Ct. 882, 88 L.Ed. 1148 (1944).

[20]   WINNIFRED FALLERS SULLIVAN, THE IMPOSSIBILITY OF RELIGIOUS FREEDOM, NEW ED. (Princeton Univ. Press 2018).

BASIC CONCEPTS   23

the breadth of what can be considered religion may become so broad that they are hard to apply in any coherent fashion. A third approach, which is to include any belief system that includes belief in the supernatural—whether viewed as divine or not—in the definition of religion, may be a potential compromise. This approach, however, may simply combine the under-inclusiveness of the strict definition approach and the potential over-inclusiveness of the broader approach. After all, why is the supernatural necessary for a belief to be religious? This question goes to the core of the debates over the demarcation point between religion and non-religion and does not have a commonly agreed upon answer.

As a result of this quagmire, this book will consider the question of what counts as religion only contextually within a given system on a given legal issue, and even then, only if the question of what counts as religion is relevant to how that system has addressed the legal issue. This section has hopefully given you a sense of the fraught nature of trying to define religion. Legal systems have provided several approaches, all of which are arguably flawed. This is not, however, necessarily the fault of the legal systems, but rather a realistic result of the practical and metaphysical difficulties inherent in trying to define religion.

2. Religious freedom

2.1 Introduction

Religious freedom is a broad term that encompasses issues such as the ability to freely practice one's religion free from government interference, the ability to receive exemptions from generally applicable laws that interfere with or burden religious practices, the ability of religious entities to govern their affairs free from government interference, and freedom from religious discrimination. Sometimes religious freedom claims impact the rights of others. These situations receive a great deal of media attention, but most religious freedom claims do not impact the rights of others. Moreover, in many legal systems religious freedom claims cannot be successful if granting the requested religious accommodation would negatively impact the rights of others. This chapter will address the usual situations where religious freedom claims do not interfere with the rights of others, as well as those where a claimed right to religious freedom might interfere with the rights of others.

2.2 Who is protected

One of the first questions that arises in the religious freedom context is: Who has the right to religious freedom? In many systems, including the US, Japan, and many EU countries, individuals and religious entities such as churches, synagogues, mosques, temples, and religious nonprofits have a right to religious freedom. In the US, at least under federal law, for-profit entities also have the right to religious freedom. This is a bit odd when compared to many other legal systems, such as those of many EU member states and Japan, and, as will be discussed below, it can lead

RELIGIOUS FREEDOM   25

to some of the situations in which an assertion of religious freedom may interfere with the rights of others. Yet, given recent events in the US, it is an important issue to address. The following subsections will address the categories of those who have religious freedom rights in various systems.

2.2.1 Individuals

Individuals' rights to religious freedom are a core element of many systems. How far these rights go vary, as discussed in later sections of this chapter. Yet, the right of an individual to practice religion is a core element of religious freedom.

In systems such as the US and Japan, individual understandings of religious practices are a core basis for the right. In these systems, courts do not judge whether an individual's asserted belief or practice is religiously 'correct'. The only question is whether an individual is asserting a sincerely held religious belief or practice.

Thus, in a famous case in the United States, a Jehovah's Witness successfully sued for unemployment benefits when he was moved from a job at a foundry that produced raw materials for weapons to a job that directly manufactured weapons. The employee asked to be fired and was ultimately denied unemployment benefits. The US Supreme Court held that as long as the employee's belief was sincerely held, it did not matter whether all Jehovah's Witnesses or Jehovah's Witnesses generally shared the plaintiff's belief that producing raw materials for weapons is acceptable but directly working to manufacture weapons is not.[1]

2.2.2 Religious entities

'Religious entities' is a category that incorporates a wide range of entities. The most obvious are houses of worship such as churches, synagogues, shrines, mosques, temples, and so on. Moreover, in some religions houses of worship are connected to a larger religious entity such as a denomination. These entities, whether formally hierarchical or not, are also religious entities.

---

[1]   *Thomas v Review Board of the Indiana Employment Security Div.*, 450 U.S. 707 (1981).

26 ADVANCED INTRODUCTION TO LAW AND RELIGION

Of course, religious entities take on many other roles and forms as well. Religious nonprofits such as soup kitchens and homeless shelters, primary and secondary schools, colleges and universities, orphanages, hospitals, and volunteer groups are also religious entities. Given the wide array of contexts in which these entities function, and the fact that they are more likely to serve the general public, religious nonprofits raise a number of questions that houses of worship qua houses of worship do not. These will be discussed later in this chapter.

2.2.3 For-profit entities

In many legal systems for-profit entities do not have a right to religious exemptions from generally applicable laws. In the United States, however, the US Supreme Court held that closely held for-profit entities (and perhaps other for-profit entities) have a right to an exemption from federal law under the Religious Freedom Restoration Act (RFRA). In *Burwell v Hobby Lobby*,[2] decided in 2014, the Court held that the term "persons" under RFRA includes closely held for-profit entities.

RFRA only applies to federal law and policies, but several states have followed suit under state RFRAs or other state laws. Some other states do not include for-profit entities as "persons" protected under their state RFRAs, and of course some states do not have RFRAs or similar legal protections.

The protection of for-profit entities under RFRAs has led to a great deal of controversy and has made it more likely that religious freedom claims may conflict with others' rights.[3] Thus, there have been a number of cases involving wedding vendors who do not want to provide services for same-sex marriages. In these cases, whether the state has a RFRA or similar law that protects for-profit entities can make a difference in outcomes. In *Masterpiece Cakeshop v Colorado Civil Rights Commission*,[4] the US Supreme Court held that states cannot discriminate against religious businesses, but that those businesses may still be bound by neutral state

---

[2] *Burwell v Hobby Lobby*, 573 U.S. 682 (2014).

[3] See, e.g., FRANK S. RAVITCH, FREEDOM'S EDGE: RELIGIOUS FREEDOM, SEXUAL FREEDOM, AND THE FUTURE OF AMERICA (Cambridge Univ. Press 2016).

[4] *Masterpiece Cakeshop v Colorado Civil Rights Commission*, 584 U.S. ___, 138 S. Ct. 1719; 201 L. Ed. 2d 35 (2018).

antidiscrimination and public accommodation laws that are neutrally enforced. These sorts of legal conflicts show no sign of slowing down as of this writing in 2022.

2.3 Exemptions from general laws

Often laws are made without considering the impact they may have on religious practices. This is especially true when laws have a negative impact on religious minorities. In many situations lawmakers may not be aware of the religious practices of religious minorities, or, even if aware, may not think of the impact a law may have on religious practices. We are dealing here with laws that are not designed to discriminate, but rather that are generally applicable but may place a substantial burden on religious practices. When this happens, the question arises whether religious individuals or entities have a right to an exemption from the law to the extent that it burdens their religion.

When analyzing this question, two subquestions arise. First, what counts as a "generally applicable" law? Second, if religious exemptions are available to generally applicable laws, how are the rights to an exemption weighed against any potentially conflicting government interests or public interests more generally?

2.3.1 General applicability

At the most basic level, a law of general applicability is a law that applies to society at large. Therefore, laws of general applicability do not make distinctions between religions or between religion and non-religion. Obviously, if a law targets religion or makes distinctions based on religion, it would not be generally applicable.

Yet, in a system like that of the United States, where many religions interact with federal, state, and local law, the concept of general applicability raises many questions. In recent years the US Supreme Court has clarified the concept. First, generally applicable laws must be neutral so that they do not discriminate based on religion. Discrimination can arise based on the language of a law, the function of a law, the structure of a law, or the implementation of a law.

In 2021 the US Supreme Court decided *Fulton v City of Philadelphia*,[5] where the Court clarified that a law is not generally applicable if exemptions are available to anyone, whether religious exemptions or other sorts. In *Fulton*, this included the authority to grant an exemption under the law even if an exemption had never been granted. Whether or not religious exemptions to generally applicable laws are available depends on the legal system involved. As the next section will show, depending on the system, religious exemptions may be mandatory, permissive, or unavailable. In the US the answers may be different in different states and under different aspects of federal law.

2.3.2 Exemptions

There are many approaches to and theories about providing exemptions to laws of general applicability. Theoretical approaches range from those suggesting that giving religious exemptions favors religion to those arguing that religious exemptions are necessary in pluralistic, religiously diverse societies so long as there is some mechanism in place to balance exemptions against social needs. How to analyze that balance, and where the proper tipping point between exemptions and social needs lies, is itself the subject of a great deal of theoretical debate.

One issue that has been addressed by many scholars, and which has commanded a range of approaches, is the question of a coherent demarcation point between religion and nonreligion. The question of where religion ends and where nonreligious philosophical or other commitments begin is a fraught one. After all, if there is a right to religious exemptions, the vexing question of what counts as religion is naturally important. If religious exemptions are mandatory barring an adequate interest to deny an exemption, the religious nature of a claimed exemption matters.

Yet, as Winnifred Fallers Sullivan and others have explained defining religion in any coherent way that suggests a clear demarcation point is problematic.[6] Relatedly, any artificial line that favors traditional religions creates equality problems. Still, in systems where religious freedom is legally protected there remain strong arguments for protecting it despite

---

[5] *Fulton v City of Philadelphia*, ___ U.S. ___ (June 2021).
[6] WINNIFRED FALLERS SULLIVAN, THE IMPOSSIBILITY OF RELIGIOUS FREEDOM (Princeton Univ. Press, New ed. 2018).

RELIGIOUS FREEDOM   29

demarcation problems, although proceeding with caution and deference to the demarcation and definitional concerns remains important.[7]

There are vast disagreements among scholars over the proper role of, and approach to, religious exemptions. This debate has been reflected in some judicial decisions and has also impacted relevant legislation, but even then, there is disagreement among judges and lawmakers over which approach is best suited to help decide what to do about religious exemptions. Yet, as is often said, courts do not have the luxury of waiting until theoretical and social disputes are settled when a case is before them. Moreover, legislators may need to, or want to, act before all the implications of a law have come into focus. This has resulted in a variety of approaches to exemptions. Here we will look at the US, Japan, and the ECHR as examples of different approaches to the question of religious exemptions.

In the US, the right to religious exemptions from general laws is not guaranteed under the Constitution but is constitutionally required under certain circumstances. Religious exemptions are required under some state constitutions and by the federal Religious Freedom Restoration Act (RFRA) and the federal Religious Land Use and Institutionalized Persons Act (RLUIPA). Moreover, many states have their own RFRAs. In all of these situations the right to an exemption can be overcome if the government has a compelling interest in denying the exemption and denying the exemption is the least restrictive way to meet that compelling interest.

Assume the following three scenarios. First, a law requires that animals killed for consumption be killed by a stun bolt. Such a requirement would prevent kosher and halal slaughter. Kosher and halal butchers and those who can only consume kosher or halal food request an exemption. Second, a law requires that adoption agencies that contract with the government not discriminate based on LGBTQ status among a variety of other factors. A Catholic adoption agency requests an exemption for placement with same-sex couples and points to an existing exception under the law for placement decisions to consider the language(s) spoken by potential parents and adoptees. Third, during an uncontrolled pandemic the government prevents gatherings of people who do not live in

---

[7]   *See, e.g.,* Frank S. Ravitch, Masters of Illusion: The Supreme Court and the Religion Clauses (NYU Press 2007).

the same household because it is clear that gatherings of any sort lead to transmission and often death or serious injury. A church requests an exemption, and the government argues that it has a compelling interest in denying the exemption.

In the US, the answer to the first scenario may vary depending on where those requesting the exemption live. The outcome of the second situation will depend on whether the law allows other exceptions, and the outcome in the third situation will depend on a variety of factors. Let's explore each in turn.

In the first situation the slaughter law is a law of general applicability with no exceptions. Thus, under current US constitutional law there would be no right to an exemption, although the government could give an exemption if it so chose. Yet, that is not the end of the question. If the law were a federal law, RFRA would apply. The substantial burden this law places on Jews and Muslims would need to be justified by a compelling interest, and denying an exemption specifically for kosher and/or halal slaughter would need to be the least restrictive means to meet that compelling interest. The government might have a compelling interest in animal rights, but kosher slaughter, at least, requires a killing that may be more humane than a stun bolt. Moreover, a less restrictive means of meeting the compelling interest for halal slaughter would be to allow a humane method that is consistent with halal rules.

Of course, most laws of this sort are state or local laws, so where the law is located could have a major impact on the outcome. In states where the state constitution requires religious exemptions to generally applicable laws, the compelling interest test is usually applied. The same is true in states that have state RFRAs. Yet, in states where neither of these options are available it is possible that no exemption would be required, although in most places one might be given in the law itself. This latter point—the availability of permissive accommodations—would be of little solace where such an accommodation is not granted. Lest one think this is purely hypothetical, consider that similar laws have been proposed in Western Europe and raised the very questions raised by this hypothetical under national laws, EU law, and the ECHR. Moreover, a similar law was proposed but rejected in San Francisco. The practical reality is that in the short term, at least, it is unlikely that a law like this would pass in the US without exceptions for kosher and halal slaughter, but were such a law to be enacted, whether there is a right to a religious exemption may depend on what state passed the humane slaughter law.

The second situation is somewhat similar to the situation in the *Fulton* case mentioned above. However, in this case an adoption agency is seeking an exemption, rather than a foster care agency. Moreover, in this situation the language exemption in the law is already being used rather just being potential. Thus, it would seem that under the *Fulton* approach the adoption agency in this case would be entitled to an exemption under the Free Exercise Clause of the United States Constitution because there is another exemption available under the law, unless the government can meet the strict scrutiny test. Once one exemption is available, religious exemptions cannot be denied without a compelling interest and narrow tailoring.

In this scenario the government might be able to meet strict scrutiny if there are no other adoption agencies available or the Catholic agency refuses to refer same-sex couples to other agencies or back to the government entity for referral to other agencies. In these scenarios, denying an exemption to the agency may be the only way to avoid discrimination against same-sex couples under the antidiscrimination law. Yet, so long as there are other options available for same-sex couples and the Catholic agency is willing to refer same-sex couples, the government would not meet strict scrutiny because, as explained in *Fulton*, there may not be a compelling interest in denying an exemption to this specific agency where other options exist—and even if there were a compelling interest in denying the exemption, allowing referral is a less restrictive way to meet that compelling interest. Significantly, if the antidiscrimination law did not have any exemptions or potential exemptions there would be no right to a religious exemption under the United States Constitution and the analysis would be similar to that in the first hypothetical; that is, the right to an exemption could vary from jurisdiction to jurisdiction.

The third situation is a variation on the COVID-19 restriction cases decided by the US Supreme Court in 2020 and 2021. The outcomes in those cases varied based on a number of factors that will be addressed in section 2.5. This situation is different, however, because here there is not even plausible evidence of discrimination, since religious entities were treated the same as all other entities.

32   ADVANCED INTRODUCTION TO LAW AND RELIGION

There would be no right to a religious exemption pursuant to the United States Constitution under these facts, but there might be a potential right to an exemption under a RFRA or state constitution. For present purposes we will assume this is so. Therefore, the main question is whether the government has a compelling interest in denying the religious exemption and whether the denial is the least restrictive way of meeting that interest. Under these facts it seems the government would win. Preventing death and serious harm during a pandemic is one of the most compelling interests imaginable and in this situation the pandemic is so deadly that only members of the same household can see each other in person. The church is not being treated any differently than other entities and under the facts any gathering, including a religious gathering, could become a superspreader event. Therefore, denying the exemption is the least restrictive way to meet the government's compelling interest.

How might these cases come out in other systems? Japan is one of the most interesting systems to explore the question of religious exemptions to generally applicable laws. Article 20 of the Constitution of Japan provides a constitutional right to religious freedom. Often the best test of a right occurs when an unpopular or little-known group asserts the right. A petty bench of the Japanese Supreme Court dealt with just such a situation.[8]

In 1996 a petty bench of the Japanese Supreme Court upheld the right of a Jehovah's Witness to receive an exemption to a public technical college's requirement that students participate in kendo (a Japanese martial art often practiced using bamboo swords).[9] The court held that the right to freedom of religion would be weak were religious practices not protected. On the other hand, the court explained that the government does have an interest in enforcing general rules, but that alone is not enough to deny a religious exemption. The government must have an important reason to deny an exemption and when granting an exemption, the government may require the person granted the exemption to meet alternative requirements so long as those requirements are not significantly more

---

[8]   The Japanese Supreme Court has two types of benches, the Petty Bench and the Grand Bench. The Petty Bench has five Justices decide a case, while the Grand Bench consists of all the Justices.

[9]   Kobe Technical College Case, Saikou Saibansho [Sup. Ct.] Mar. 8, 1996, 1995 Gyo-Tsu no. 74 (Second Petty Bench).

burdensome than the general requirement. In the Kendo case the student had offered to do computer modeling, write a paper, and/or take notes on kendo. The school had the choice to require those or impose its own requirements in order for the student to receive the exemption.

There is debate among Japanese legal scholars as to whether this case was decided under the Constitution of Japan or the education laws, which were also a focus of the decision. There is a strong argument that both influenced the decision, but that the right to an exemption expressed by the court exists under both the constitution and the relevant education laws. In support of this argument, it should be noted that a number of government entities in Japan have followed the court's approach in areas outside of education.

This case is significant because in Japan religion is not as much of a focus as it is in the West—although it would be a vast oversimplification to say that Japan has low religiosity, given the merging of religion and culture in many aspects of Japanese life. I have referred to this as "religion as culture" (宗教の文化 Shuukyou no Bunka). Moreover, groups and individuals that proselytize are often seen as intolerant because in Japan one can easily have no religion or subscribe to a combination of Buddhist, Shinto, and/ or other religions. Also, in Japan, social conformity is quite important. Yet, in the *Kobe Technical College* case, the plaintiff was a member of an unpopular religion but won the right to a religious exemption in a society that values conformity. So, how would our hypothetical situations play out in Japan?

Unlike in the United States, where there are numerous free exercise of religion cases at all levels of the judiciary, Japan has a much smaller number of cases and cases in general are not as important as the civil code and other legislation. Thus, in analyzing the above hypotheticals under Japanese law a bit more guesswork is needed as to how they might be analyzed, but the process of doing so will help show the differences and similarities between the Japanese and US models.

A law like the one in the first hypothetical would be highly unlikely to arise in Japan, for a variety of reasons that go far beyond the focus of this book, but assuming such a law did arise it is likely that the kosher and halal butchers and individuals who eat kosher and halal meat would receive exemptions, although they may face bureaucratic hardships in

34 ADVANCED INTRODUCTION TO LAW AND RELIGION

initially attaining the exemptions. Why is this the case? Unlike the United States, where there is no constitutional right to a religious exemption to generally applicable laws, in Japan that right seemingly exists, albeit with some limitations as mentioned above. Unless the government has a strong reason for denying the exemption, the exemption should be granted. Animal cruelty might be a strong enough reason, so there is no guarantee of a win for those seeking the exemption, but conformity with a general law would not by itself be an adequate basis for an exception. Certainly, other requirements could be made if an exemption is granted, such as minimizing any pain an animal suffers consistent with the relevant religious practices, which is already the point of kosher slaughter.[10] Moreover, the Religious Juridical Persons Act (宗教法人法 *Shuukyou Houjin Hou*) might provide additional rights and protections for religious entities to be able to distribute kosher or halal food and might also protect the butchers depending on their relationship with a religious organization(s). Yet, one issue in Japan is the difference between rights that exist and the understanding and application of legal exceptions by local, regional, and national bureaucrats. Sometimes it can be hard to get exceptions to any law or rule, even when one is legally entitled to them, without jumping through a lot of hoops. Ultimately, however, an exemption would likely be available and enforceable.

As in the US, many cities and prefectures in Japan protect against discrimination based on LGBT status, while some others do not. As of early 2022 there is no strong national antidiscrimination law that covers LGBT rights in Japan,[11] but there has been significant movement toward passing one. As of 2022, three district courts have come to conflicting results about the right to same-sex marriage—as opposed to civil union—in Japan. In 2021 a court in Sapporo ruled that denying same-sex marriage violated the Constitution of Japan, but in June 2022 a court in Osaka ruled the opposite and then in November 2022 a court in Tokyo did the same. There are several other cases pending in other courts and the issue

---

[10] In kosher slaughter there cannot even be one minor nick on the knife used, the slaughter must occur with one strike, and that strike must sever specific arteries that carry blood to the brain, therefore minimizing pain.

[11] In Japan the term LGBT is used more than LGBTQ. Gender nonconformity is in some ways more accepted in Japan than in Western countries, but in other ways social conformity might create issues for a gender nonconforming individual in some corporate or other settings. It may be that LGBT in Japan includes all aspects of LGBTQ, but this is currently unclear.

will likely have to be resolved by national legislation. Still, many cities and prefectures recognize a right to civil unions so the second hypothetical could still arise in Japan even before there is a national right to same-sex marriage.

How would the second hypothetical play out in Japan? Unlike the US, where there have been significant disputes between socially conservative religious groups and LGBTQ rights, in Japan resistance to LGBT rights is generally not based in religion, but rather cultural conservativism. Moreover, it is unlikely that, for example, a Buddhist adoption agency would deny access to same-sex couples or seek an exemption from a law that prohibited discrimination based on same-sex civil union or marital status.

Yet, the Roman Catholic Church and some socially conservative Protestant groups do have a footprint in Japan, including in the charity sector. This author is unaware of any conflicts like those in the United States, and it is quite likely that such conflicts would be settled in Japan by referrals to other agencies without litigation. Yet, if it were to go to court, two principles in Japanese law would come into conflict: first, the principle of freedom of religion; second, the principle that rights should be exercised for the public welfare. This second principle, which is set forth most clearly in Article 12 of the Constitution of Japan, could require that the right to an exemption be subject to the public welfare. This, would of course, raise the fraught question of which is better for the public welfare: denying an exemption and perhaps having the adoption agency close rather than violate its religious tenets; or allowing discrimination against same-sex couples that violates local antidiscrimination laws. In a way, this more directly brings front and center the conflicts that arise in the adoption context. One could see this issue going either way, but my guess—and it is only a guess—is that the adoption agency might win on the narrowest basis possible, given the risk of the agency closing and the children being harmed.

The discussion about public welfare above would provide a clear answer to the third hypothetical. The power of the government to mandate closures or limitations on people or juridical people such as corporations and non-profit entities in Japan even during an emergency is an open question, but assuming such a power existed and was used, the church would almost certainly lose. In this scenario, given a pandemic and the

36 ADVANCED INTRODUCTION TO LAW AND RELIGION

risk to public welfare such gatherings pose, any right to an exemption that might exist in normal circumstances would not apply. Moreover, the sort of tortured discrimination reasoning used by the US Supreme Court in *Roman Catholic Diocese of Brooklyn v Cuomo*,[12] which equates churches to supermarkets and the like, would be highly unlikely to occur in a Japanese government setting or Japanese court setting. Further, rights under the Religious Juridical Persons Act would not be helpful to a religious entity in this context.

It may be easiest to predict how the ECHR would decide the second and third hypotheticals. Yet, the first hypothetical is not at all hypothetical in Europe, and in light of a recent—and highly questionable—decision by the European Court of Justice (ECJ),[13] the ECHR may soon decide the exact issue presented in that hypothetical. Here, the ECJ upheld a Belgian law that required stunning animals before slaughter. Similar laws exist in many places throughout Europe, but some, such as the UK law, provide an exception for kosher or halal slaughter. This is because the stun bolt used renders the animal unkosher or unhalal and therefore the law essentially prevents religious Jews and Muslims from having kosher or halal meat.

As explained above, the outcome in the US would clearly be the opposite of the ECJ decision and it is likely the same would be true in Japan. To make matters worse, Belgium has a strong history of antisemitism, and more recently also anti-Islamism, and there was some evidence that animal rights was not the only factor behind the law.[14] In addition to those concerned about animal rights, the Belgian law was supported by nationalist, anti-immigrant lawmakers. Thus, the ECHR may have a basis to address the case under both Article 9 and Article 14. The focus here will be on Article 9.

---

[12] *Roman Catholic Diocese of Brooklyn v Cuomo*, 529 U.S. ___, 141 S.Ct. 63, 208 L.Ed.2d 206 (2020).

[13] CJEU 17 December 2020, Case C-336/19, *Centraal Israëlitisch Consistorie van België and Others*.

[14] Recently, the parliament for the Brussels-Capital region of Belgium scrapped the law proposing the ban. Therefore, at least from the day of that vote, June 17, 2022, kosher and halal slaughter remain legal in the Brussels-Capital region of Belgium, but not in Belgium's other regions.

Article 9 protects not just the right to hold a belief, but also the right to manifest that belief. Article 9 §2 provides a qualification to the right to manifest belief, namely, limitations on manifestation of religion must be "prescribed by law" and must be "necessary in a democratic society in the interests of public safety, for the protection of public order, health or morals, or for the protection of the rights and freedoms of others." This list *is* exhaustive.

The decision by the ECJ acknowledged the interference with Jewish and Muslim rights but held, against the recommendation of the ECJ Advocate General, that the Belgian law met the "prescribed by law" and "necessary in a democratic society" requirements of the European Charter of Fundamental Rights (which is generally interpreted using ECHR concepts) in denying an exemption for kosher and halal slaughter. Specifically, the court held that the law met an "objective of general interest recognized by the European Union, namely the promotion of animal welfare." In doing so the ECJ seemed to minimize the religious impact of the law and some of the nationalist elements behind the law. Yet, Belgium did assert a strong case from an animal rights perspective, so the issue was not whether the Belgian government had an interest, but whether it outweighed the interference with core religious practices. The ECJ decided that it did, but how the ECHR might rule remains an open question as of this writing.

Even when a law meets the "prescribed by law" and "necessary in a democratic society in the interests of public safety, for the protection of public order, health or morals, or for the protection of the rights and freedoms of others" requirements under the ECHR, it must show that the national law is justified in principle and proportionate. Under ECHR precedent this means that "there must be no other means of achieving" the national interest "that would interfere less seriously with the fundamental right concerned."[15] The ECHR does give member states a good deal of deference in these cases, but that deference is not total. Of course, governments are free to give exemptions that do not interfere with the rights of others even when not required to do so.

---

[15]   *Biblical Center of the Chuvash Republic v Russia* (ECHR, 1st Sec. June 12, 2014) at Section 58.

A number of member states such as Germany and the UK have provided exceptions to their stunning rules for kosher and halal slaughter, albeit strictly enforced exceptions. This might help the Belgian Jewish and Muslim communities' arguments. The Belgian government's strongest argument under the ECHR might be that denying a religious exemption to the stunning regulation is necessary in a democratic society for the protection of health and morals, and perhaps public order. These may seem weak arguments given the interference with core religious manifestations and the fact that a narrow exemption would still allow the member state to protect its interest in general. Moreover, kosher slaughter, at least, was designed to be more humane than other slaughter, and halal slaughter can be carried out in a similar fashion. Therefore, allowing a narrow exception would be more justified in principle and proportionate than not allowing an exemption. Here the differences in EU law and ECHR law, which the ECJ has historically minimized, come into clear focus, because the ECJ did not minimize the differences in this case. Also, given some of the evidence of discriminatory intent by the Flemish-region government where the situation began, the ECHR might address this situation under Article 14 rather than Article 9. This latter possibility is beyond the scope of this section.

The second and third hypotheticals would be decided in favor of the government because in both cases the rights to manifest religion interferes with the rights of others. In the second hypothetical, the right to exclude same-sex couples from adopting would interfere with the rights of those couples and the ECHR has repeatedly held that when the right to manifest religion interferes with the rights of others, states have great leeway to deny exemptions. Interfering with the rights of others is one of the specific limitations allowed by the text of Article 9 §2 on the manifestation of religion and granting an exemption for a religious practice that interferes with the rights of others would facilitate that interference.[16]

The third hypothetical is even easier to answer under the ECHR. Under that hypothetical an exemption would interfere with the rights of others, including possibly causing death. Moreover, denying an exemption would also serve the other specific limitations allowed by Article 9 on the

---

[16] See, e.g., *Eweida and Others v The United Kingdom* (ECHR, 4th Sec. Jan. 15, 2013); Pichon and Sajous v. France (ECHR Oct. 2, 2001); *Van Den Dungen v The Netherlands* (ECHR Feb. 22, 1995).

right to manifest religion. Specifically, prohibiting events that may spread infections during a pandemic serves the interests of public safety, preventing harm to the public order, and preventing a threat to public health. Unless the member state banned online services, or perhaps outdoor socially distanced and masked services, there would be no less restrictive way to protect the above interests than prohibiting indoor gatherings during a pandemic. If, however, a member state banned online meetings, the religious entities would almost certainly prevail. If the member state banned outdoor socially distanced and masked services it would be a closer call, but during a pandemic the member state would have the benefit of the doubt on all the specific limitations on manifestation of religion provided under Article 9 §2. Therefore, if there were any scientific basis for limiting outdoor, socially distanced and masked services, the member state is likely to prevail. If there is no such evidence, however, it is possible the church might win. Yet, it would be possible that, given the potential damage spread of the disease could cause during a pandemic, and the deference given to member states, even in the latter situation, the member state might win.

2.4 Rights versus rights: when religious freedom claims conflict with the rights of others

Religious exemptions usually don't conflict with the rights of others, but on occasion they do—for example, in situations where a wedding vendor refuses to provide services for a same-sex wedding based on objection to being complicit in something that goes against the vendor's religion, or situations where a pharmacist refuses to provide what are commonly referred to as morning-after pills based on a religious objection to being complicit in something that goes against the pharmacist's beliefs.

In some systems, when religious freedom conflicts with the rights of others, the rights of others prevail. This is especially clear in the European system, where the ECHR has specifically held that a religious exemption cannot justify refusing services to others, especially by for-profit entities.[17] While the outcome of these sorts of situations in Japan is less clear given that they rarely arise there, it is likely that for-profit entities would not be

---

[17]   *Id.* (all cases).

40   ADVANCED INTRODUCTION TO LAW AND RELIGION

able to assert religious exemption claims and, even if they could do so, exemptions that impact the rights of others would not be available.[18] The same is true in many other systems.

The situation in the US, however, is different, at least at the federal level. At the state level there are a web of approaches, discussed below. The US Supreme Court has implicitly, at least, sided with those asserting a right to religious exemptions under the federal Religious Freedom Restoration Act (RFRA) even when doing so could harm the rights of others. More recently the Court has sided with religious entities seeking not to be bound by local COVID-19 restrictions, although, as explained below, these cases were not framed as exemption cases.

In *Burwell v Hobby Lobby*,[19] the Court held that companies, one of which had more than 13,000 employees, could deny certain contraceptive coverage under their health plans because they had a sincere belief that those forms of contraceptives are abortifacients and that covering them would make the employer complicit in their use. In the United States most health insurance is gained through one's employer, so the holding meant that employees who were insured by the companies' health plans would not be covered for certain IUDs and what is commonly called the "morning after pill" under their health insurance. The holding, however, was not so limited and it is possible that it might apply to other forms of birth control or other medical treatments.

The Court held that RFRA mandated an exemption to a provision of the US Affordable Care Act which required insurance plans to pay for contraceptive coverage. The Act had exceptions for religious entities, but not for for-profit companies. The Court first had to decide whether closely held for-profit entities are covered by RFRA and whether it is possible to substantially burden the religion of a for-profit corporation, or at least for

---

[18]   Article 20 §1 of the Japanese Constitution which protects religious freedom has never been interpreted to give for-profit entities a right to exemptions. The Japanese Religious Juridical Persons Act (Shuukyou Houjin Hou 宗教法人法), which gives certain protections to religious organizations that register under the act, specifically defines "religious organizations" in a manner that would exclude for-profit businesses that are not part of a religious entity. Moreover, Japanese laws, court decisions, and culture are generally reluctant to grant rights that have a negative impact on others.

[19]   573 U.S. 682 (2014).

RELIGIOUS FREEDOM   41

a closely held for-profit corporation. Prior to *Hobby Lobby* most courts had held that the answer to these questions was "no." The *Hobby Lobby* Court held, however, that the answer to both questions is "yes." The reasoning for these parts of the decision has been heavily criticized by some, including this author, but supported by others. This part of the decision is not particularly relevant to the discussion in this Advanced Introduction. The key is that, once the questions were answered in this way, if the government action substantially burdens religion, the government must provide a religious exemption unless it can show that denying the exemption is the least restrictive way to meet a compelling government interest.

Once the Court held that a for-profit entity could have its religion substantially burdened, this element was easy to meet. The ACA required that non-complying entities pay hefty recurring fines that would have bankrupted the companies. Thus, there is little question that there was a substantial burden placed on the companies' religion.[20]

The Court assumed arguendo that mandating contraceptive coverage is a compelling government interest and thus did not analyze the question. As Justice Ginsburg pointed out in dissent, this enabled the Court to sidestep questions about the burden an exemption might create for others, namely, those denied insurance coverage for the contraceptives. Thus, the Court never explicitly held that an exemption can interfere with the rights of others. In fact, the Court attempted to address this concern in the narrow tailoring part of the decision, but as will be seen, that part of the decision left open the possibility that the rights of others could be harmed.

---

[20] A great deal of commentary and several courts of appeal decisions prior to *Hobby Lobby* had argued that substantially burdening a for-profit company's religion was impossible because the company is basically just a piece of paper registering it as such with the state. Thus, beyond profit-making, the argument was that these entities had no beliefs and no religion to substantially burden. Even for closely held companies, some commentators and courts argued that the owners are not the company any more than the employees or customers are. Therefore, they viewed closely held companies holistically, such that the owners' religion could not define the company's religion if it could somehow have religion. The first position was somewhat undermined by the Court's decision in *Citizens United v Federal Election Commission*, 558 U.S. 310 (2010), which held that for-profit entities had free speech rights enabling them to express political and social values. The *Hobby Lobby* Court relied on *Citizens United* when addressing the for-profit entity aspects of the case.

The Court held that there are more narrowly tailored options than denying the exemption. For example, the Court pointed to the fact that religious nonprofits had the option to certify that they objected to providing contraceptive coverage and the insurer was then required to provide coverage and seek reimbursement from the government. The Court found this to be a less restrictive alternative to denying an exemption.

Yet, this would require the employees to access the care available through the government-funded program after the company opt-out, which would at the very least require proof that the employee is indeed employed by the company receiving the exemption. This might cause the employees' personal information and decisions to be exposed to their employer. More importantly, there is no guarantee that government will be consistently willing to fund this coverage. Therefore, *Hobby Lobby* presents a situation where there is some conflict between what the Court said and what the Court did. That is, the Court said that there were more narrowly tailored options that would still ensure coverage, but as a practical matter those options could lose support or funding at any time and could also put female employees in the position of having their personal medical choices known to their employer in order to access the coverage.

This may have been less problematic given the limited scope of the companies' objections in *Hobby Lobby*, but other companies might object to providing any form of birth control, and this could place a significant financial burden on female employees who need birth control both for a variety of health conditions and/or for birth control itself. Moreover, the Court later held that requiring religious nonprofit employers to certify their objections to providing certain contraceptive coverage also violated religious freedom, and this would seemingly apply to objecting for-profits as well, after *Hobby Lobby*. As a practical matter it is unclear whether RFRA would support a religious exemption that harmed others as a matter of law, but the Court has interpreted it in a way that minimizes the burden on others almost out of existence.

The COVID-19 cases were not framed as exemption cases. Rather, they were framed as cases about unconstitutional discrimination in violation of the Free Exercise Clause of the United States Constitution. Yet, a finding in favor of the religious entities would effectively exempt them from the state and local COVID-19 restrictions they were contesting. The outcomes in these cases went both ways. For example, in *Roman Catholic*

Diocese of Brooklyn v Cuomo,[21] the Court granted injunctive relief against a New York order creating occupancy limits of 10 or 25 people in areas hard-hit by COVID-19. The Court held that because secular businesses, including grocery stores, were not subject to the same limits, the limits on churches and other houses of worship were discriminatory. Therefore, it violated the Free Exercise Clause.

On the other hand, in *South Bay United Pentecostal Church v Newsom*,[22] the Court denied injunctive relief to a church that challenged a statewide order limiting attendance at indoor events. The Court did not find discrimination in this case. Other cases followed a similar pattern of divided outcomes and opinions.

These cases certainly do not stand for the proposition that religious exemptions that harm others are mandated. Yet, as a practical matter, this is the effect of some of the COVID-19 decisions. In the New York case the state produced significant evidence that indoor church services featuring singing and prolonged periods indoors could spread COVID-19, and it was well established that one infected person could spread COVID-19 to others. Some have argued that the Court substituted its judgment for that of the state health authorities once it found that the state's categories discriminated against religion. The Court also did not accept New York's argument that its orders were the least restrictive means for protecting public health during a pandemic.

It remains unclear as a legal matter whether exemptions to generally applicable laws that harm others are valid under RFRA or the Free Exercise Clause, but as a practical matter the Court, along with some lower courts, has allowed exemptions that at least potentially interfere with the rights of others. Thus, unlike in Europe and many other places, it is at least possible at the federal level in the US for exemptions that harm others to be granted. At the state level, however, there is no one approach.

At the state level a number of factors are relevant to whether an exemption that might harm the rights of others is available. The most common situation where this has arisen is when a for-profit entity such as a wedding vendor refuses to provide services for a same-sex marriage. The first

---

[21]   529 U.S. ___, 141 S.Ct. 63, 208 L.Ed.2d 206 (2020).
[22]   590 U.S. ___, 140 S.Ct. 1613, 207 L.Ed.2d 154 (2020).

question is whether there is a state law providing protection against discrimination by public accommodations for the general public and/or the LGBTQ community. In most jurisdictions there is at least a general public accommodation law which mandates service to all. Thus, issues arise when someone seeks a religious exemption from providing services that they have a duty to provide under the public accommodation law. These situations are more pronounced and problematic when the person or entity is seeking the exemption for a for-profit activity. The US Supreme Court acknowledged this in *Masterpiece Cakeshop v Colorado Civil Rights Commission*,[23] when the Court noted that in most circumstances a state would be expected to be able to apply its public accommodation laws neutrally against any business that refuses to serve citizens, but that it is not appropriate to order a clergy member to perform a marriage to which that clergy member objects.

Thus, as a general matter, religious exemptions are not mandated at the state level as a matter of federal law; however, as explained earlier, many states have state RFRAs or interpret their state constitutions to require exemptions unless the state can meet strict scrutiny. This is where the question becomes interesting and difficult. Assuming the state does apply its RFRA or state constitutional protection to for-profit entities—something that not all states do—there is a potential conflict between the rights of members of the LGBTQ community and the right to a religious exemption. This could arise in the context of other antidiscrimination laws as well as other sorts of laws, such as state laws mandating contraceptive coverage. So how would this play out?

So far there have been a few cases where state RFRAs conflicted with public accommodation laws, and in a number of the cases the state courts found that the state has a compelling interest in enforcing its antidiscrimination laws and that enforcing them generally is the most narrowly tailored way to meet the interests protected by those laws. This result is not universal, and the results could be quite different in different states. Also, context matters. A religious entity might be treated differently than a business when it comes to claiming a religious exemption, and in fact many states exempt religious entities from public accommodation laws.

---

[23]   584 U.S. ___, 138 S. Ct. 1719 (2018).

RELIGIOUS FREEDOM   45

Thus, in many places around the world a religious exemption is unlikely to be given when doing so would harm the legally protected rights of others. This may not be true, however, in the US. At the time of this writing, in summer 2022, the answer in the US at the federal level is unclear, while at the state level the answer can vary from state to state.

2.5   Discrimination against religion

The question of exemptions is an important topic for religious freedom. Another important topic is the question of discrimination against religion. This topic can range from situations where government targets certain religious entities with negative treatment to situations where employers discriminate based on religion. The employment context, where there are numerous national, regional, and local laws at play, is beyond the scope of this book except where the employer is itself a religious entity. That topic will be addressed in Chapter 4 in dealing with the doctrine of church autonomy, which includes a discussion of ministerial exceptions. This section will focus on situations where government action is alleged to be discriminatory against religion.

This issue has become increasingly important in the US, where the Supreme Court has recently expanded a doctrine that had historically required clear evidence of discrimination, but which no longer does. The US situation will be the main focus of this section, but the US is not the only place where government discrimination against religion has been found unconstitutional or otherwise illegal.

For example, in *Religionsgemeinschaft der Zeugen Jehovas and Others v Austria*[24] and *Savez crkava "Riječ života" and Others v Croatia*, the ECHR

---

[24]   No. 40825/98, July 31, 2008 at paragraph 92: "the obligation under Article 9 of the Convention incumbent on the State's authorities to remain neutral in the exercise of their powers in this domain requires therefore that if a State sets up a framework for conferring legal personality on religious groups to which a specific status is linked, all religious groups which so wish must have a fair opportunity to apply for this status and the criteria established must be applied in a non-discriminatory manner."

46 ADVANCED INTRODUCTION TO LAW AND RELIGION

found potential discrimination against religious groups.[25] In the first case the ECHR found the imposition of a ten-year waiting period for new religious groups to achieve the status of a "religious society" under Austrian law to be discriminatory. The status of "religious society" carried many benefits which groups without that status were denied. In the second case, the ECHR found discriminatory the Croatian government's establishment of a special relationship favoring some religious groups while refusing to come to an agreement with other religious groups that would have allowed them to perform certain religious ceremonies and would have given legal recognition to marriages performed by their clergy.

Significantly, however, the expansion of the nondiscrimination doctrine in the US has been vast and goes beyond what most systems are willing to accept. This is, in part, because recent decisions by the US Supreme Court have overridden the rights of other citizens and state interests in not favoring religion. Moreover, decisions by the US Supreme Court over the past five years have allowed the Court to find discrimination against religion in situations where the evidence of discrimination was highly questionable.

In 1993 the US Supreme Court decided a case called *Church of the Lukumi Babalu Aye v City of Hialeah*,[26] which involved discrimination by the city of Hialeah, Florida against a Santeria church. The city created a law that was gerrymandered to ban only Santeria animal sacrifice and city officials as well as residents made highly discriminatory statements against Santeria at public meetings. The Court held that the law was targeted at the Church of Lukumi Babalu Aye and that it discriminated against that church and the Santeria faith. Because the Court found that the law is discriminatory under the Free Exercise Clause of the US Constitution, the city could only win if it met strict scrutiny.

Strict scrutiny requires that the government have a compelling interest and that what the government did is narrowly tailored to meet that

---

[25] No. 7798/08, Dec. 9, 2010: "Accordingly, the only question for the Court to determine is whether the difference in treatment had 'objective and reasonable justification', that is, whether it pursued a 'legitimate aim' and whether there was a 'reasonable relationship of proportionality' between the means employed and the aim sought to be realized."

[26] 508 U.S. 520 (1993).

compelling interest. The city asserted that the law was created to serve the compelling interests of preventing animal cruelty and protecting sanitary waste disposal. The Court rejected both of those interests because the city allowed hunting, fishing, pest control including killing rodents and other animals, other kinds of religious slaughter and other practices that could be viewed as cruel to animals. Regarding the concerns over sanitation, the city allowed restaurants to leave out garbage that included rotting food and there was also no evidence that the Church of Lukumi Babalu Aye disposed of waste in an unsanitary fashion. Therefore, the asserted compelling interests were inadequate, and the Court held that even if they were adequate, the banning of animal sacrifice in toto was not narrowly tailored to meet those interests because there were other less restrictive ways to protect the city's asserted interests.

This case stood as the only US Supreme Court case to find actionable discrimination under the Free Exercise Clause until 2017. Lower courts and many commentators generally understood the case to mean that actionable discrimination under the Free Exercise Clause requires some kind of animus-based discrimination whether that be demonstrated by open animus or laws that targeted a particular religion(s).

In 2004, the Court decided *Locke v Davey*.[27] The Court held that the state of Washington could deny a scholarship under a state college scholarship program to a student who wanted to use it for devotional theology (training to become a clergy member). The State of Washington asserted concerns that it would violate its duties under the state constitution if it funded training to become a clergy member and Mr Davey challenged the decision under the Free Exercise Clause of the US Constitution. The Court held that there is "play in the joints" between free exercise and establishment concerns and that because the state did not deny scholarships to religious colleges or for religious studies generally, the denial for training to become a clergy member was within this "play in the joints." The Court also explained that concerns over funding the clergy have a long history in the US and were a core reason behind the Establishment Clause to the US Constitution and many state constitution non-establishment provisions.

---

[27]   540 U.S. 712 (2004).

48   ADVANCED INTRODUCTION TO LAW AND RELIGION

It was not until *Trinity Lutheran v Comer* in 2017[28] that the Court again found a Free Exercise Clause violation based on discrimination against religion. In that case Trinity Lutheran ran a school that applied for playground chips made from recycled material under a Missouri state program. The Missouri state constitution had a no-aid provision for religious schools, so the state denied Trinity Lutheran's request. Trinity Lutheran sued under the Free Exercise Clause. The Court held that denying Trinity Lutheran the ability to compete for access to the playground chips simply because of its religious status was a violation of the antidiscrimination principle required by the Free Exercise Clause and could only be justified if the state could meet strict scrutiny. The court held that the state could not meet strict scrutiny in the case because the state's interest in denying access for religious entities to compete in a program that supplies recycled playground chips was not compelling, as the chips would simply protect children on the playground and did not promote religion.

Importantly, in footnote 3 the Court explained that playground chips do not have a religious use and that the decision did not address funding that could be used for religious purposes. This likely led to Justice Kagan joining the opinion and Justice Breyer concurring in the judgment. Justice Gorsuch wrote a concurring opinion where he disagreed with the majority opinion's apparent religious status/religious use distinction. His opinion was an indication of things to come.

Just three years later, in *Espinoza v Montana Dept. of Revenue*,[29] in a 5–4 decision the Court held that denying parents who send their kids to religious schools access to a tuition assistance program violates the antidiscrimination principle of the Free Exercise Clause.[30] The state Department of Revenue had denied access to the program for those who would send their children to religious schools under the "no-aid" provision of the state constitution. This provision precluded the state from providing any kind of financial support to religious schools.[31] While the tuition

---

[28]   582 U.S. ___ (2017).

[29]   591 U.S. ___, 140 S. Ct. 2246 (2020).

[30]   This was so despite the fact that the Montana Supreme Court struck down the entire tuition assistance program rather than just the application of it to religious schools.

[31]   These no-aid-to-religious-schools provisions are common in state constitutions, but some share a dark history of anti-Catholic bias which was

RELIGIOUS FREEDOM 49

assistance program at issue in the case was quite limited, the holding goes well beyond the specific program at issue in the case and strikes down any "no-aid" to religious schools provision contained in a state law or state constitution unless the state can meet strict scrutiny.

The Court held that denying access to any government program based on religious status imposes "special disabilities" on religion and is discrimination that violates the Free Exercise Clause. The concern about religious uses of government funds mentioned in footnote 3 of the *Trinity Lutheran* case was either forgotten or ignored by the majority opinion. The Court applied strict scrutiny to the state's decision to deny access to the tuition assistance program for those who would use the tuition assistance at religious schools. The Court rejected the state's asserted compelling interest of promoting a stronger separation between government and religion than is applied under the federal Establishment Clause, especially after *Zelman v Simmons-Harris*[32] (a case that will be discussed in detail in section 5.1 below). The state interest was not compelling enough to justify a violation of the federal constitution's Free Exercise Clause.

Therefore, after *Espinoza* even a state's interest in not subsidizing religion is unconstitutional when the state denies access to a program based on religious status, unless the state can meet strict scrutiny, which seems highly unlikely given the Court's reasoning in *Espinoza*. This is a significant expansion of the antidiscrimination concept from *Lukumi Babalu Aye*, but the Court expanded the concept further in a 2022 case called *Carson v Makin*[33] and in some of the 2020–21 COVID-19 cases.

In *Carson v Makin*, decided in June 2022, the Court dramatically expanded the decision from *Espinoza*, which was itself a dramatic expansion of the doctrine from *Trinity Lutheran*. In *Carson* the Court held that Maine must provide vouchers to religious schools if it does so for secular private schools. Maine provided tuition reimbursement to private schools in areas of the state that did not have enough students to support public

---

addressed in some of the opinions in the *Espinoza* case. Interestingly, the Montana "no-aid" provision which had been re-passed at the 1972 state constitutional convention was based on an earlier constitutional provision that shared in the troubling history of anti-Catholic bias but which, when re-passed with slight changes in 1972, reflected no such bias.

[32] 536 U.S. 639 (2002).

[33] ___ U.S. ___ (2022).

schools. Maine has vast expanses of territory without major towns or cities. Maine provided the vouchers to any school, secular or religious, as long as those schools did not teach religion or require students to engage in religious exercises. The Court abandoned the status/use distinction from *Trinity Lutheran* and *Espinoza* and held that Maine must fund religious schools that teach religion and even proselytize if it funds other private schools, unless Maine could meet strict scrutiny. Despite Maine's geographic situation and lack of public schools in some areas the Court held that Maine's interest in not funding religious education and/or proselytization was not an adequate interest to justify the ban.

Therefore, from now on, to avoid violating the Free Exercise Clause of the US Constitution, states must include religious schools (including those that proselytize and directly teach religion) in any funding program open to non-religious schools or even to religious schools that do not mandate the teaching of religion. This is so regardless of the state's interest in not promoting religion and regardless of a state constitution's antiestablishment provision(s). The only way to avoid funding religious schools would be to have no funding for private education at all, which in Maine is not a practical option given the state's geography. Thus, in the span of five years the Court has completely changed the understanding of the antidiscrimination principle of the Free Exercise Clause, from primarily protecting against intentional discrimination which was mostly targeted at religious minorities to primarily protecting the religious interests of those with large enough populations to support their own religious schools.

Still, the Court went even further in a series of cases in 2020 and 2021 dealing with the COVID-19 crisis. The outcomes in the COVID-19 cases went both ways, but in *Roman Catholic Diocese of Brooklyn v Cuomo*[34] the Court further expanded the antidiscrimination principle under the Free Exercise Clause to a context where public health was at stake. In that case the Court granted an injunction against a New York state order creating occupancy limits of 10 or 25 people in areas hard hit by COVID-19. The Court held that because secular businesses, including grocery stores, were not subject to the same limits as houses of worship, the limits on houses of worship was discriminatory in violation of the Free Exercise Clause.

---

[34]   529 U.S. ___, 141 S.Ct. 63, 208 L.Ed.2d 206 (2020).

Significantly, in *Cuomo* the state produced significant evidence that indoor church services with singing and prolonged periods inside could spread COVID-19 and it was well established that one infected person could spread COVID-19 to others. New York state health authorities drew lines based on the type of gathering using the science available at that time amid a pandemic. Yet, the Court held that the decision to include houses of worship in a category that included theaters while many stores remained open was discriminatory. It is a fair argument to say that the Court substituted its judgment for that of the state health authorities, or at the very least recharacterized the decision of state health authorities as discriminatory rather than science-based, when it found that the state's categories discriminated against religion.

Since the state was found to have discriminated against religion, strict scrutiny applied. The state certainly has a compelling interest in protecting public health, but the Court held that New York did not use the least restrictive means for protecting public health when it categorized houses of worship as a whole, rather than based on square footage, specific ventilation systems, and so on. Yet, the state did not consider those factors when categorizing theaters and the like, either. Regardless of what one thinks of the *Cuomo* decision, it is a further expansion of the antidiscrimination concept under the Free Exercise Clause, because it allowed the Court to decide what comparison groups to take into account in finding discrimination in the first place.[35]

2.6 Discrimination by religion

Questions about legal protections for discrimination by religion have come to the fore in the US and elsewhere recently. As was explained above, these issues can arise when a religious entity seeks an exemption to a general law prohibiting discrimination in access to services, places, or

---

[35] This was not the first case in which the Court hinted this was possible. In *Masterpiece Cakeshop v Colorado Civil Rights Commission*, 584 U.S. ___, 138 S.Ct. 1719 (2018), the Court based its finding of discrimination on its own assessment of the facts including a comparison to a situation that a concurring opinion and the dissenting opinion found to be substantively different from the situation that gave rise to the case.

52 ADVANCED INTRODUCTION TO LAW AND RELIGION

goods. These issues can also arise when people or entities seek religious exemptions to public safety laws. Many democratic systems, such as the ECHR (and also the ECJ)[36] and the Canadian legal system,[37] to name just two, have decisions that preclude protection for religious freedom claims when those claims involve interference with important rights of others.

The US has become a bit of an outlier on this issue, as the discussion of the *Hobby Lobby* case and the COVID-19 exemption cases above demonstrates. There are also a slew of cases involving wedding vendors denying services to members of the LGBTQ community in various states throughout the US.[38] The outcomes in these cases can vary based on whether states have broad or narrow public accommodations laws, whether they have state RFRAs, and if so to whom these laws apply. Much of this dynamic was discussed in prior sections and will not be rehashed here. The key is that the US Supreme Court has issued opinions that point in each direction. On the one hand, *Hobby Lobby* and some of the COVID-19 cases suggest that religious freedom claims can overcome the rights and safety of others.[39] Yet, dicta in the *Masterpiece Cakeshop* decision suggests that states are free to apply their antidiscrimination laws neutrally even when doing so requires that wedding vendors and others may be required to violate their religious conscience. Still, given changes in the makeup of the US Supreme Court since 2018, when *Masterpiece Cakeshop* was decided, it is unclear how such cases might be decided if they reached the current US Supreme Court on the issue of whether denying an exemption to

---

[36]   *Eweida and Others v The United Kingdom* (ECHR, 4th Sec. Jan. 15, 2013); *Pichon and Sajous v France* (ECHR Oct. 2, 2001); *Van Den Dungen v The Netherlands* (ECHR, Feb. 22, 1995).

[37]   *Law Society of British Columbia v Trinity Western University*, 2018 SCC 32, [2018] 2 S.C.R. 293.

[38]   See, e.g., FRANK S. RAVITCH, FREEDOM'S EDGE: RELIGIOUS FREEDOM, SEXUAL FREEDOM AND THE FUTURE OF AMERICA (Cambridge Univ. Press 2018).

[39]   The most recent case, *Fulton v City of Philadelphia*, 593 U.S. ___ (2021), involved a situation where a Catholic charity was not required to recognize same-sex couples as being married in order to become foster parents, but the situation in the case was a bit different from *Hobby Lobby* and the COVID-19 cases, where the potential harms to the rights and safety of others were potentially severe. In *Fulton* there were numerous other providers to which the Catholic charity was willing to refer LGBTQ married couples and the charity did not exclude single members of the LGBTQ community from becoming foster parents for the children in its care.

a public accommodation law for someone asserting a religious freedom claim violates the Free Exercise Clause.

3. Government support for religion: public education

3.1 Introduction

Government support for, or promotion of, religion is a multifaceted issue involving everything from government financial aid to religious entities to government displays of religious symbols. Issues such as public school prayer and public religious ceremonies are also common concerns. Yet, the sorts of issues that arise vary widely among legal systems. Some systems, such as the United Kingdom, have an established church. Others, such as a number of European systems, have a system for recognizing various religions and providing benefits to recognized religions. Still others, such as the United States, Canada, and Japan, have varying degrees of separation between government and religion that prohibit government from favoring any specific religion or religion generally. Still others, such as France, have systems that promote secularism as a public good.

Each of these systems have succeeded and failed to achieve their ideals to a certain degree. Yet they demonstrate the rich tapestry of possibilities in democratic societies as they grapple with the question of whether government should support religion and, if so, how much support should be given. As was true in the previous chapter, a detailed discussion of the many systems around the world is beyond the scope of this book. The primary focus will be on how different types of systems address specific issues such as those involving religion in schools, religion on public property, private versus public expressions of religion, funding for religious entities, tax exemptions for religious entities, legislative prayer, and what can loosely be called civil religion or ceremonial deism.

GOVERNMENT SUPPORT FOR RELIGION: PUBLIC EDUCATION   55

These issues will be split across three chapters. This chapter will focus on religion in schools. Chapter 4 will focus on public property, private versus public expressions of religion, legislative prayer, and ceremonial deism. Chapter 5 will focus on funding and tax exemptions for religious entities.

These chapters will not address systems like that of the UK, which have an established religion, but rather will focus on systems such as those in the US and Japan that aspire to some level of separation between government and religion, systems like some within the European Union that recognize and provide certain benefits to religion(s) or a subset of religions, and systems like that of France, which aspire to official secularism. As will be seen, aspirations and ideals have not always been met in these systems, but the many ways in which government and religion may come into contact in complex societies make achieving any ideal a fraught endeavor. Rather, the aspirations and ideals of various systems may serve as loose templates that are sometimes followed and sometimes not. The US provides a great example of this, as the concept of strong separation between church and state went from being a hallmark of US Establishment Clause jurisprudence through the 1990s to a hollow shell of its former self by 2019. Yet, until 2022, the US still maintained a significant level of separation when viewed in a global context. As will be seen in section 3.2 and in Chapters 4 and 5, two cases decided by the US Supreme Court in 2022 have brought the separation concept to its lowest point in 75 years.

3.2   Public schools

When discussing the law related to schools, the focus will be on religious exercises, religious symbolism or religious teaching in public schools. Support and funding for private schools will be addressed in Chapter 5. Moreover, questions such as equal access to school facilities for religious clubs and private religious speech in public schools will be addressed both in this chapter and in Chapter 4.

3.2.1   Public school prayer

There are a variety of approaches to public school prayer worldwide, ranging from a school-sponsored daily prayer to consideration of school-sponsored prayer as unconstitutional. The US situation is perhaps

56   ADVANCED INTRODUCTION TO LAW AND RELIGION

among the most famous and has spawned many cases. Recent decisions by the US Supreme Court have caused major shifts in the law under the Establishment Clause but organized public school prayer is one area in which the results, at least, may remain the same.

Regardless of the legal system addressed in this section, the focus will be only on public schools or their equivalent. Of course, countries have a variety of structures for public schools, common schools, and the like. Discussion of the structures of these systems is beyond the scope of this book. The focus is on organized prayer in schools that are open to all students in a given area and are not totally privately owned or sponsored (in some systems schools may be run by private entities but still fall under the public school rubric, such as some schools in the UK or charter schools in the US).

Within these sorts of schools there are a variety of different approaches to organized prayer. Contrast, for example, the UK and the US. In the UK, prayer and some other religious activities have been mandated for many years.[1] In the US, by contrast, organized public school prayer has been repeatedly found unconstitutional.[2] EU countries take a variety of approaches from mandating daily prayer (usually with exemptions for students/families who object to participation in the prayer) to not having organized prayer at all.

In Japan, organized school prayer qua prayer has not been an issue but, pursuant to Ministry of Education guidelines applying the Act on National Flag and Anthem Law (国旗国歌法) passed in 1999, there have been numerous instances of students and teachers refusing to sing the national anthem, *Kimigayo*, which praises the emperor and harkens back to the ardent nationalism and militarism that the current Japanese Constitution and many Japanese people have come to reject. Cases of teachers refusing to sing the anthem have made it to the Japanese Supreme Court but have been analyzed on freedom of conscience/academic freedom grounds

---

[1]   Recently, there have been challenges to these requirements which have either settled in the complainant's favor or led to exceptions to the general requirements.

[2]   *Engel v Vitale*, 370 U.S. 421 (1962); *Abington Tp. v Schempp*, 374 U.S. 203 (1963); *Lee v Weisman*, 505 U.S. 577 (1991); *Santa Fe Indep. School Dist. v Doe*, 530 U.S. 290 (2000).

GOVERNMENT SUPPORT FOR RELIGION: PUBLIC EDUCATION   57

rather than separation of politics and religion grounds. Yet, the national anthem itself could be considered to have religious content, so there could be an interesting case to be made that forcing anyone to sing it would violate Article 20 of the Japanese Constitution if doing so is viewed as a religious act (violating Article 20 §2 and/or 3) and/or if someone objected to singing it on religious grounds (violating Article 20 §1 and 2).

Significantly, the US has been the locus for some of the most detailed and legally clear decisions on public school prayer. This is partially because in the US public school prayer is a constitutional question and partially because the question of religion in public schools has been front and center in the US culture wars since at least the 1960s. Before the 1960s, cases involving public school prayer were decided under state constitutions, and in a number of these cases public school prayer was found to violate a state constitution. These decisions, however, only applied in the relevant state, so there was no national rule on public school prayer until the US Supreme Court addressed the issue in *Engel v Vitale* in 1962 and *Abington Township v Schempp* in 1963.[3]

These cases both held that organized public school prayer violated the Establishment Clause of the First Amendment and thus is unconstitutional. *Schempp* also held that daily Bible reading is unconstitutional. Both decisions also noted that students are free to pray privately by themselves.[4] In *Schempp* the Court set forth a test for determining whether a public school religious exercise violates the Establishment Clause of the First Amendment to the United States Constitution. The test looked at the purpose and the primary effect of the religious activity. The Court held:

> If either [the purpose or effect] is the advancement or inhibition of religion, then the enactment exceeds the scope of legislative power as circumscribed by the Constitution. That is to say that, to withstand the strictures of the Establishment Clause, there must be a secular legislative purpose and a primary effect that neither advances nor inhibits religion.[5]

---

[3]   370 U.S. 421 (1962); 374 U.S. 203 (1963).
[4]   It was implicit in this that students are free to pray quietly and privately with likeminded students. This is, however, different from the concept of "voluntary, student-initiated prayer" found unconstitutional in *Santa Fe Indep. School Dist. v Doe*, discussed below. As will be seen, that sort of prayer is neither truly voluntary nor student-initiated. Importantly, however, truly private prayer has always been protected in the public schools.
[5]   *Schempp* at 222.

58   ADVANCED INTRODUCTION TO LAW AND RELIGION

This test became part of the famous *Lemon* test derived from the Court's 1971 decision in *Lemon v Kurtzman*.[6] The *Lemon* case and the *Lemon* test were overturned in June 2022 in *Kennedy v Bremerton School District*.[7] *Kennedy* did not overturn *Engel* or *Schempp*, however, so it is unclear whether the *Schempp* approach will remain applicable in the school prayer context. This is one of the many questions that have arisen as the Court has overturned longstanding precedents, either directly or implicitly, in recent years. The *Kennedy* case will be addressed in Chapter 4. For now, this book will assume that the *Schempp* test may still be applicable to organized public school prayer situations, but with the caveat that no precedent involving culture war issues—no matter how longstanding—is clearly safe under the current Court. Readers should understand that US constitutional law in the context of religion can turn on a dime with the current Court, and therefore it is important even year to year to see what precedent remains binding and how.

Significantly, however, even if the *Schempp* test goes by the wayside with the *Lemon* test, there remain two other tests that have been applied to school prayer cases and at least one of those—the indirect coercion test—still seems to command a majority of the Court. Also of importance is the fact that daily organized school prayer may be directly coercive depending on how it is analyzed.

In the years following the *Engel* and *Schempp* cases it was clear that organized public school prayer is unconstitutional, but questions arose about situations such as prayer at public school graduations. Prayer at public school graduations was the focus of the Court's 1991 decision in *Lee v Wesiman*.[8] In *Lee*, the Court held that a nonsectarian prayer delivered by a clergy member at a public school graduation violates the Establishment Clause. Rather than using the *Lemon* test, or the endorsement test that came to the fore in the late 1980s and will be discussed further below, the Court held that the prayer was coercive because of the pressure to participate placed on students. Specifically, the Court held:

> These dominant facts mark and control the confines of our decision: State officials direct the performance of a formal religious exercise at promotional

---

[6]   403 U.S. 602 (1971).
[7]   ___ U.S. ___ (2022).
[8]   505 U.S. 577 (1991).

GOVERNMENT SUPPORT FOR RELIGION: PUBLIC EDUCATION   59

and graduation ceremonies for secondary schools. Even for those students who object to the religious exercise, their attendance and participation in the state-sponsored religious activity are in a fair and real sense obligatory, though the school district does not require attendance as a condition for receipt of the diploma [...] The government involvement with religious activity in this case is pervasive, to the point of creating a state-sponsored and state-directed religious exercise in a public school. Conducting this formal religious observance conflicts with settled rules pertaining to prayer exercises for students, and that suffices to determine the question before us.[9]

The key was that the religious exercise was being conducted at an event that is exceptionally important for students—a graduation—at which there is peer pressure and social pressure to conform. Therefore, the majority opinion stated there was no need to address the *Lemon* and endorsement tests. Concurring Justices, however, did apply those tests and found that the graduation prayer violated those tests as well. This would be reflected in the Court's next school prayer case, decided in 2000.

By 2000, three tests had been used to analyze public school prayer: the *Lemon* test, the endorsement test, and the indirect coercion test from *Lee*. In *Santa Fe Indep. School District v Doe*,[10] the Court applied all three of these tests to a policy that potentially enabled prayer before high school football games. The school district in the case had a history of flouting the Establishment Clause and had already been found by lower courts to have violated the Establishment Clause by having a student chaplain policy, religious assemblies, and a number of other brazenly unconstitutional practices. The policy allowing for students to select by majority vote a student speaker to make a statement before football games was the culmination of several attempts by the school district to support prayer.

The district argued that because the students elected the speaker who delivered the statement, any prayer given would be private speech that could not be attributed to the school for Establishment Clause purposes. The argument was that this so-called voluntary, student-initiated prayer was not state action and was protected by the Free Speech Clause. The flaws in this argument were obvious and the Court made short shrift of them. First, the school created the policy that allowed the vote and students were aware of that fact. Second, for there to be protected free speech

---

[9]   *Id.* at 586–87.
[10]   530 U.S. 290 (2000).

60 ADVANCED INTRODUCTION TO LAW AND RELIGION

the time before football games would have to be a "limited public forum," where, at a given time and/or location, free speech or at least free speech by a designated group (in this case students) would be allowed without content discrimination. Yet, on its face, the school policy created content discrimination by only allowing the majority's representative to speak. By limiting the possibility of counter-speech or any other speech the district was violating the Free Speech Clause if indeed, as the school district implicitly asserted, the pre-football game speech time was a limited public forum. The free speech argument was an attempt to avoid analysis under the Establishment Clause, but since the free speech argument had no merit, the Court turned to analysis under the Establishment Clause.

The Court held that because the prayer would occur at a school-sponsored event attended by school officials and students, surrounded by school regalia and banners, and so on, the prayer endorsed religion. To be an unconstitutional endorsement of religion a government activity must have the purpose or effect of creating insiders and outsiders along religious lines and endorse religion from the perspective of a reasonable observer familiar with the history and context of the challenged government activity. Given the history of the district's promotion of sectarian Christian religion, the divisiveness in the community, and the nature of the location and event at which the prayer would occur, the Court found that the policy unconstitutionally endorsed religion. The Court also held for similar reasons that the policy had an unconstitutional purpose to promote religion in violation of the *Lemon* test.

Finally, the Court held that the policy violated the indirect coercion test (and for students who had to be there, such as band members, players, cheerleaders, there may have been direct coercion). The main question under the indirect coercion test was whether football games satisfy the important event criteria that graduations obviously satisfied. The Court held that being able to attend high school football games, which are important social and community events in the US, should not be dependent on participating even indirectly in a prayer. Peer pressure would also make it harder for students to always arrive late to avoid the prayer or to avoid standing or implicitly supporting the prayer.

To date, public school prayer is one of the few subjects in law and religion where the Court has consistently come to the same result, albeit under a variety of tests. At this point it is unclear what impact the *Kennedy* case

GOVERNMENT SUPPORT FOR RELIGION: PUBLIC EDUCATION 61

decided in 2022 will have on this. *Kennedy* will be addressed in Chapter 4. For now, it should be noted that *Kennedy* overturned the *Lemon* test and probably the endorsement test as well, but it is unclear if the latter might still apply to school prayer that is endorsed by the school. The indirect coercion test remains intact at the moment, albeit through a combination of Justices in the *Kennedy* majority and dissents.

3.2.2 Creationism in public schools

The promotion of creationism and/or intelligent design in the public schools is not a problem unique to the US, but it has occupied more legal focus in the US than anywhere else. While attempts have been made to promote creationism and/or intelligent design in Australia and elsewhere, the number of state or local laws and attempts by school boards seeking to promote creationism and/or intelligent design is especially high in the US. Of course, there are countries where teaching or promoting creationism would not be an issue because those countries have no antiestablishment principle. Moreover, in some countries, such as Japan, the idea of promoting creationism or intelligent design in science classes would be unthinkable because they have no serious scientific support. This section, however, will focus on the US as an example of a legal system where these issues arise *and* have constitutional significance.

Throughout the early and mid-twentieth century, several state courts in the US addressed laws either prohibiting the teaching of evolution or promoting creationism in the public schools. These cases were decided under state constitutions or other state laws. The US Supreme Court's first decision addressing creationism in the public schools was in the 1968 case *Epperson v Arkansas*.[11] In that case the Court held that an Arkansas law prohibiting the teaching of evolution in its public schools and universities violated the Establishment Clause of the First Amendment to the United States Constitution. The Arkansas law in question made it a crime to teach evolution in public schools and universities and exposed any teacher who did so to dismissal and potential criminal liability. In 1965 the Little Rock school district recommended a new biology text, which included instruction on evolution. A biology teacher in the district, Susan Epperson, realized that if she taught the evolution section in the new book she would potentially be subject to dismissal and criminal liability under

---

[11]   393 U.S. 97 (1968).

62 ADVANCED INTRODUCTION TO LAW AND RELIGION

the state law, even though the school district had approved the text. She believed that teaching the material was in the best interest of her students and she sued the state, asking the courts to declare the law unconstitutional and therefore unenforceable against her and other teachers.

The Court agreed with Ms Epperson. It held the law was unconstitutional because it did not have a secular purpose. The Court held that the Arkansas law was designed to prevent evolution—and only evolution—from being taught in public schools because evolution was antithetical to a particular religion:

> [T]here can be no doubt that Arkansas has sought to prevent its teachers from discussing the theory of evolution because it is contrary to the belief of some that the Book of Genesis must be the exclusive source of doctrine as to the origin of man. No suggestion has been made that Arkansas' law may be justified by considerations of state policy other than the religious views of some of its citizens.[12]

Moreover, the law could not be defended on the ground that it was "neutral" as to religion. If a law was found to be "neutral" in regard to religion, courts ordinarily found (and still likely would find today) that the law does not violate the Constitution. Significantly, the argument that the Arkansas law was religiously neutral was squarely rejected by the Court because while the law did not mandate the teaching of creationism or the teaching of human origins generally, it excluded only discussion of evolution. It did not preclude discussion of creationism so long as evolution was not discussed. Therefore, only the religiously disfavored view was excluded, and the law was unconstitutional. This, however, was not the last time the Court addressed a question about promoting creationism in the public schools.

On July 20, 1981, Louisiana Governor David C. Treen signed the "Balanced Treatment for Creation-Science and Evolution in Public School Instruction" act into law. The law was sponsored by state senator Bill Keith, who introduced a related bill in June 1980. The stated purpose of the law was to promote academic freedom, but it did so by requiring that "creation science" be taught whenever evolution is taught in Louisiana public schools. There was no explicit prohibition on teaching creation science before the law was enacted, and under the law there was

---

[12]   *Id.* at 107.

GOVERNMENT SUPPORT FOR RELIGION: PUBLIC EDUCATION   63

no requirement that either creation science or evolution be taught. The only requirement was that teachers teach creation science if they teach evolution.

The Louisiana law was an example of what came to be known as "balanced treatment laws." These laws were supported by the creation science movement, a predecessor to the intelligent design movement. The creation science movement evolved mostly from what are known as "old earth creationists." Old earth creationists believe the Earth may be quite old, but that complex life forms—especially human beings—were placed here by God in their present form. Some "young earth creationists" were also involved. Young earth creationists take the timeline in the Bible literally and date the creation of the Earth and humanity to about 6,000 years ago.

The legal arm of the creation science movement was focused on gaining public acceptance for creationism, and especially to gain access to public education science classes. By couching creationism in scientific terms, creation scientists hoped to be able to win court battles over the constitutionality of teaching creation science in public schools. One of the major strategies creation science advocates employed was "balanced treatment" laws like the one in Louisiana. Creation scientists argued that these laws were designed to promote academic freedom and free speech. The Louisiana law was challenged in federal court shortly after it was signed. The Supreme Court issued its decision on the matter—*Edwards v Aguillard*—in 1987.[13]

In *Edwards*, the Court held that the Louisiana law was unconstitutional because its purpose was to promote a religious concept, creation science, and not to promote academic freedom. *Edwards* was a major defeat for the creation science movement and was also a defining moment for what would become the intelligent design movement.

The *Edwards* Court focused exclusively on whether the Louisiana "Balanced Treatment Act" had a valid secular purpose. After looking at the language of the Louisiana "Balanced Treatment" law, the statements of Senator Keith who introduced it, statements by other legislators and government officials, and statements by those who testified before the legislature on the bill, the Court held that the purpose of the law was to

---

[13]   482 U.S. 578 (1987).

64   ADVANCED INTRODUCTION TO LAW AND RELIGION

promote creationism and to favor the views of certain Christian denominations. The Court did not accept the state's argument that the law was designed to promote academic freedom. Rather, it held that the law could not serve the purpose of promoting academic freedom because the law limited rather than expanded academic freedom.

Also weighing heavily against the claim of a valid secular purpose were the facts that the law's proponents spoke in explicitly religious terms and that creation science posits that human beings were placed on Earth by a supernatural creator. Moreover, the Court found that the law was designed to counter evolution with creationism "at every turn," which served the religious beliefs of certain religious groups. To make matters worse for the state's asserted secular purpose, the law provided support for additional creation science teaching materials but not for the development of additional evolution materials, and it provided protection for teachers who taught creation science but not for those who taught evolution (even though, under the law, if one was taught the other had to be taught).

Significantly, the Court rejected the argument that creation science does not promote religion simply because it claims to be science. This point became especially important to the few courts that have addressed intelligent design:

> The preeminent purpose of the Louisiana Legislature was clearly to advance the religious viewpoint that a supernatural being created humankind [...] Senator Keith's leading expert on creation science, Edward Boudreaux, testified at the legislative hearings that the theory of creation science included belief in the existence of a supernatural creator.[14]

The *Edwards* decision, and the defeat of "balanced treatment" acts in other courts,[15] became an impetus for what would eventually become the intelligent design movement. In fact, when one looks at the basic tenets of the intelligent design movement it seems clear that intelligent design was designed, in part, to avoid some of the problems that doomed "creation

---

[14]   *Id.* at 591.
[15]   "Balanced treatment" acts were also defeated in *Daniel v Waters*, 515 F.2d 485 (6th Cir. 1975) (finding Tennessee "balanced treatment" law unconstitutional) and *McLean v Arkansas Bd. of Educ.*, 529 F. Supp. 1255 (E.D. Ark. 1982) (same for Arkansas act).

science" in the courtroom. After all, a major goal of the intelligent design movement is to introduce intelligent design in public schools.

Anyone who believed that the debate over teaching creationism in the public schools would die down after *Edwards* failed to learn from the events after *Epperson* that led to the "creation science" movement. As creationism begat creation science, soon after *Edwards* creation science would beget intelligent design. The move from creationism to creation science had caused a rift among creationists while providing creation scientists with new legal ammunition. The move from creation science to intelligent design did the same.

There are two overarching components to intelligent design: first, exploiting gaps in evolutionary biology and attacking evolutionary biology generally; second, trying to demonstrate the designer through the complexity of living organisms. The end goal of both of these tactics is to overthrow scientific materialism and what intelligent design proponents call "naturalism." Naturalism, according to these proponents, is the idea that natural forces explain what we see in the world and in living organisms, and that the world and the organisms in it came about through purely natural (that is, no-higher-power) mechanisms. Interestingly, this is a straw-man argument. One can accept naturalism and the mechanisms said to support it without denying a higher power. In fact, the famed biologist Kenneth Miller wrote extensively about this in *Finding Darwin's God*.[16] As that book explains, many people of faith can accept what intelligent design proponents call "methodological naturalism," which is just a fancy term for the idea that natural processes have given rise to much of what we see in the world around us. Naturalism is not inherently inconsistent with faith, nor does it preclude the theological notion of God as designer. For people of faith who accept scientific evidence, naturalism may simply suggest that the natural mechanisms observed and documented by scientists are the work of God. The latter point, of course, is beyond scientific proof and thus would not be a proper subject for science classrooms even if it might be appropriate in classes on world religions or the philosophy of science.

---

[16] KENNETH MILLER, FINDING DARWIN'S GOD: A SCIENTIST'S SEARCH FOR COMMON GROUND BETWEEN GOD AND EVOLUTION (HarperCollins 1999).

66 ADVANCED INTRODUCTION TO LAW AND RELIGION

In addition to the two key components mentioned above, a central aspect of intelligent design is the tendency to deny that the "designer" is God. This argument is central to the intelligent design movement's attempts to move into public school science curricula either through disclaimers about evolution or teaching intelligent design. Yet, when one reads about the intelligent design movement both from its supporters and opponents, it seems obvious that the designer they have in mind is God. Even if the designer is not a specific deity, intelligent design cannot escape the argument that the designer is supernatural (and thus religious rather than scientific). Because intelligent design posits that any living being as complex as the human must be designed by an intelligent force, the designer of humans would obviously be complex and thus need to be designed by an intelligent force, and so on. As a result, even if courts were to take the intelligent designers' assertions that the designer is not a specific deity at face value despite all the evidence to the contrary, intelligent design still must rely on a supernatural designer, given its underlying premise.

Intelligent designers understand this, so they also rely on an argument focused on "teaching the controversy." By this they mean that teachers, professors, public personalities, and so on should teach about the controversy between intelligent design and mainstream biology. This is a clever rhetorical move. By suggesting that there is a controversy to teach about, intelligent design proponents are attempting to legitimize their approach. Further, by suggesting that the alternative to intelligent design is mainstream evolutionary biology and that the disagreements between the two should be taught, they are able to place their approach on the same rhetorical playing field as mainstream science.

But this too is a red herring. It is a brilliant rhetorical move and a wonderful use of smoke and mirrors, but, like many other arguments made by intelligent design proponents, the argument to "teach the controversy" proves too much. The whole notion of "teaching the controversy" assumes that there is an actual controversy to teach about. From the perspective of mainstream science, there is not.

All of these arguments were analyzed by a United States district court in *Kitzmiller v Dover Area School District*.[17] In that case the district court held that the inclusion of a disclaimer favoring intelligent design in

---

[17]   400 F. Supp. 2d 707 (M.D. Pa. 2005).

classrooms, the purchase and placement of intelligent design texts in the school library, and conduct by some school board members violated the Establishment Clause of the First Amendment. The key issue in the case was whether intelligent design is religion or science. This issue was important because if intelligent design is a religious concept, then including it in science classrooms, even through a mandatory disclaimer, would violate the Establishment Clause. If intelligent design was science, however, there might be an argument that it could be included in science classes despite its religious underpinnings. If intelligent design is neither religion nor science, there is no constitutional issue because if it is not religious the Establishment Clause could not be violated. Thus, the best-case scenario for intelligent design proponents would be a finding that intelligent design is science, not religion. The best-case scenario for those opposing the school board's policy would be a finding that intelligent design is not science and is religiously based. This is in fact what the court found.

The court heard testimony from leading philosophers of science, biologists, and intelligent design proponents. After hearing all this testimony and evaluating documentary evidence, such as manuscripts of an intelligent design textbook that was virtually identical to a creation science text with "intelligent designer" substituted for God and "intelligent design" for "creation," the court held that intelligent design is not science and that it is religiously grounded. The court's holding that intelligent design is religious and not scientific was central to its reasoning under the Establishment Clause. The Supreme Court had already held in *Edwards* that religiously based theories of creation (in that case "creation science") could not be taught in public school science classes without running afoul of the Establishment Clause.

Once the *Kitzmiller* court determined that intelligent design is not science but religion, the outcome that the school board policies at issue violated the Establishment Clause was unavoidable. Adding to the obvious outcome was the remarkable behavior of some school board members. Members had threatened teachers, burned an evolution mural found in a classroom, laundered the purchase of intelligent design books for the school library through a local church, made brazenly sectarian statements in their official capacities, engaged in sectarian attacks on board members and members of the public who disagreed with them, and told lies on the stand and in depositions. Once the court had determined that intelligent design is not science and is religiously grounded, all of this bad behavior

68 ADVANCED INTRODUCTION TO LAW AND RELIGION

was simply icing on the evidentiary cake. Even without it, the policy would have been unconstitutional under the prevailing legal tests applied in similar Establishment Clause cases at that time.

The court applied the endorsement and *Lemon* tests to the school board policy. It held that the disclaimer and the other events surrounding the disclaimer (including the acquisition of intelligent design textbooks for the school library) violated the endorsement test and the purpose and effects prongs of the *Lemon* test. Thus, the school board policy violated the Establishment Clause. Because the court found that intelligent design is not science and overwhelming evidence proved that it is religiously grounded, the court held that the school board's policy violated both the purpose and effects elements of the endorsement test.

The evidence demonstrated that the purpose of implementing the policy was to endorse the majority school board members' religious views, and that there is no secular purpose that would support teaching intelligent design as science. Therefore, the policy would make a reasonable observer, familiar with the history of the policy, believe that the board was creating political and religious insiders and outsiders based on religious views. The board argued that the purpose of the policy was to promote critical thinking skills and improve science education. Certainly, exposure to different ideas and values might support teaching intelligent design in comparative religion or philosophy classes, but because the court held that intelligent design is not science, there is no secular purpose for promoting it in science classes.

The board fared no better when the court analyzed the effects of the policy under the endorsement test. The court held that because intelligent design is religious and not scientific, the effect of the disclaimer and book purchases was to endorse religion. Thus, when the policy was implemented, the disclaimer was read in classes, and intelligent design books were added to the library in a well-advertised manner, a reasonable observer would believe that such actions had the effect of endorsing religion. There was substantial evidence supporting the notion that this is exactly what happened in *Dover* when the policy was being debated and after it was passed and implemented. This same analysis essentially applied to the *Lemon* effects test. The court used the same reasoning to hold that the primary effect of the *Dover* policy was to promote intelligent design, a religious concept.

As will be explained in more detail in Chapter 4, the US Supreme Court's recent decision in the *Kennedy v Bremerton School District*[18] case overturned *Lemon* and significantly called into question the endorsement test. Assuming both of those tests are gone—although there are arguments that endorsement might survive in some situations, especially because the *Kennedy* Court failed to cite important cases using that test—evolution disclaimers such as that under the Dover policy or teaching creationism or intelligent design in science classes would likely remain unconstitutional under the indirect coercion test.

Even after *Kennedy*, it seems that at least five Justices would still be willing to apply that test, including two from the *Kennedy* majority. For the present discussion the key is that teaching creationism or intelligent design in a science class would be clearly coercive both directly and indirectly, assuming the relevant courts agreed with the *Kitzmiller* court that intelligent design is religion and not science. The school would be teaching a religious subject as science and students would be a captive audience in the classroom and perhaps for class exam/evaluation purposes. Even if the school allowed objecting students to leave the room when intelligent design was taught, students might stay due to peer pressure.

If the situation involved not teaching creationism or intelligent design in a science class, but rather reading a disclaimer as occurred in *Kitzmiller*, the result would be the same, for the same reasons. Students would still be a captive audience for a disclaimer that has religious meaning and, even if allowed to be excused, might not feel safe leaving due to peer pressure. Of course, as recent decisions by the current Court, including *Kennedy*, demonstrate, no precedent is safe with the current Court. Therefore, the above analysis of the indirect coercion test may not be the analysis the Court would apply.

3.2.3 Religious symbolism in public schools

While creationism in public school science classes has been a heavily US-focused issue, questions surrounding religious symbols in public school classrooms have primarily been an issue in Europe. Again with the caveat that the *Kennedy* case may have changed everything, the question

---

[18]   ___ U.S. ___ (2022).

70 ADVANCED INTRODUCTION TO LAW AND RELIGION

of posting religious symbols in US public school classrooms has had a clear answer for decades.

If the religious symbol is hung by the school, it is unconstitutional under a case called *Stone v Graham*,[19] which found that hanging Ten Commandments plaques in public school classrooms violates the Establishment Clause of the First Amendment to the United States Constitution. On the other hand, there are numerous cases in the lower courts in the US holding that when student art or student assignments are displayed, religious content cannot be excluded or favored. Moreover, teachers who have a religious requirement to wear religious garments or headwear such as hijabs and yarmulkas would likely be able to do so under current US law, especially if the school allows any leeway as to teachers' dress requirements, as most US public schools do.[20]

The situation in Europe, however, has been quite a bit more complex, as various countries have addressed the question in different ways and the ECHR has weighed in on several major cases, including cases from Italy, Turkey, France, and Switzerland. Given the many nations in the EU and Europe more generally, it would be beyond the scope of this book to address each country's law on this question. Therefore, the ECHR decisions can be used to understand the general overarching rules applicable in Europe. Yet it is essential to remember that there remain a range of approaches to questions about religious symbolism in public school classrooms in Europe and the ECHR opinions provide the governing law under the European Convention on Human Rights, but the ECHR lacks strict enforcement measures so it is possible that some nation states may violate ECHR rulings. An example of this mentioned in the Introduction is Russia's continued persecution of Jehovah's Witnesses.

Significantly, when evaluating the decisions by the ECHR it is important to recognize that these decisions taken together, like the recent US Supreme Court decisions, appear at the very least to favor dominant religions and disfavor religious minorities and dissenters. It is hard to

---

[19]   449 U.S. 39 (1980) (per curium).

[20]   *Fulton v City of Philadelphia*, ___ U.S. ___ (2021) (holding that if the government has created any potential exceptions to a general rule or policy, religious exceptions must be granted unless the government can meet strict scrutiny).

GOVERNMENT SUPPORT FOR RELIGION: PUBLIC EDUCATION 71

avoid the role that preconceptions play in these decisions. This has been recognized by dissenting Justices in recent US Supreme Court decisions and was also recognized by the dissenting judges in the *Lautsi* case, which will be discussed next.

The ECHR cases involve questions about teachers or students wearing religious items as well as a case involving schools posting religious symbols, namely, crucifixes. As will be seen, these cases have quite different outcomes depending on the situation. On their surface, the ECHR cases evince a failure to understand the nature of religious practices for many—and especially non-Christian—religious adherents, combined with a disregard for the impact of Europe's Christocentric practices and history on religious minorities and nonbelievers. The situation, however, is more complex, because the ECHR must decide cases from numerous countries with different legal and religious systems, and it gives a good deal of deference to national laws. Thus, there is no one-size-fits-all solution and the balance and proportionality approach required under the European Convention on Human Rights is bound to lead to what appear on the surface to be conflicting results. With that said—and writing as an outsider, given that this author's primary area of expertise is the US and Asia—critics of the ECHR religion cases make several salient points about the inherent Christocentrism in ECHR decisions, as well as about the disparate impact these decisions have on religious minorities such as Muslims and Jews. Perhaps nowhere is this clearer than the religious symbolism in schools cases. To be clear, these cases were decided under the European Convention on Human Rights and thus consider the underlying law of the specific countries involved as analyzed under Article 9 of the Convention; they therefore do not reflect the national laws of all signatory countries to that Convention.

In *Lautsi and Others v Italy*,[21] the ECHR addressed a complaint by parents whose children attended a state-sponsored school that had crucifixes in all the classrooms. The parents did not want their children to be influenced by school-promoted religion. After the school refused to remove the crucifixes, the parents sued under Article 9 and Article 2 of Protocol 1 to the European Convention on Human Rights, which protect freedom of thought, conscience, and religion and the right to education, respectively. The parents won before a panel of ECHR judges, which found

---

[21]   ECHR, March 18, 2011 (Grand Chamber).

a violation of the ECHR after which the case was appealed to the ECHR Grand Chamber. Prior to the Grand Chamber's hearing of the case there was a groundswell of support for the Italian law by countries that have a strong tradition of promoting religion in state schools, many of them in Eastern Europe. There was also significant support for the parents' position and the principle of secularism. The case essentially became a European inter-nation culture war issue.

The Grand Chamber held that neither article of the Convention was violated. As to Article 9, the Grand Chamber found that because there was no European consensus on religious symbols in state school classrooms the issue was in the "margin of appreciation" for the signatory nations, which is a form of deference to signatory states. There could be a violation of Article 9, however, if there were religious indoctrination in a state school, but the Grand Chamber held that even though crucifixes in state school classrooms in Italy give predominant visibility to the majority religion, that alone is inadequate to demonstrate indoctrination. The Grand Chamber noted that there was no evidence of compulsory education about Christianity, or of Italian school authorities being intolerant of secular students or students from religious minorities. The Grand Chamber also noted that the parents remained free to raise their children with whatever religious or secular beliefs they wished.

Of course, being an ECHR Grand Bench decision, this case raises a number of concerns addressed by scholars. First, the decision applies in all European signatory countries with similar policies, some of which, such as Poland and Hungary, have seen a rise in antisemitism (or a reemergence of latent antisemitism) as well as rampant anti-Islamism. Thus, in day-to-day life this could pose significant concerns about discrimination. This may be why the Grand Chamber mentioned that there was no suggestion in the case of compulsory religious education, religious indoctrination, or discrimination in Italy. This may have been a way to warn other signatory states that such things can be a violation of Article 9.

Second, in one of the sillier lines in the decision, the Grand Chamber refers to the crucifix as a "passive symbol"—a trope also used by the US Supreme Court on occasion: "Furthermore, a crucifix on a wall is an

GOVERNMENT SUPPORT FOR RELIGION: PUBLIC EDUCATION   73

essentially passive symbol and this point is of importance in the Court's view, particularly having regard to the principle of neutrality."[22]

This is an argument made by Italy in the case. It makes sense that advocates might try this argument, but for the Grand Chamber to accept the argument and use it in its reasoning is baffling. Calling any religious symbol "passive" or "essentially passive" goes against even basic religious, anthropological, social, hermeneutic, and semiotic understandings of religious symbols.[23]

Finally, there is a seeming disjunction between the treatment of a symbol of the dominant religion in *Lautsi* and the treatment of religious minorities in several other cases. The reasons for this might be the "secular" systems in the nations involved in the latter cases. Yet, as you will see, this does not fully explain the differences in the outcomes of the cases and at the very least leaves current ECHR law open to criticisms of favoring mainstream forms of Christianity and/or secularism at the expense of religious minorities in cases involving symbolism. In recent years, as explained above, this has also been a criticism of the US Supreme Court. We turn now to the ECHR cases involving religious minorities and symbolism in state schools.

In *Dahlab v Switzerland*,[24] a teacher who had worn a headscarf for several years without any disturbances was forced to stop wearing it based on Swiss law. The Swiss federal court upheld the decision and the case went to the ECHR, which held that she did not have a valid claim under Article 9 of the European Convention on Human Rights. The ECHR said that the decision to prevent her from wearing a headscarf was not unreasonable. The ECHR noted that the teacher is a representative of the state and taught children between four and eight years old, explaining that students of that age would be more easily influenced than older students.

One might wonder out loud how one teacher wearing a headscarf could have more of an influence on young children than the crucifixes in every

---

[22]   *Id.* at ¶72.
[23]   Frank S. Ravitch, *Religious Objects as Legal Subjects*, 40 WAKE FOREST LAW REVIEW 1011 (2005); see also FRANK S. RAVITCH, MASTERS OF ILLUSION: THE SUPREME COURT AND THE RELIGION CLAUSES at 113–41 (NYU Press 2007).
[24]   ECHR, February 15, 2001.

74 ADVANCED INTRODUCTION TO LAW AND RELIGION

classroom allowed by the ECHR in *Lautsi*. Of course, the cases are different because in *Dahlab* the state was promoting secularism and the teacher filed the complaint while in *Lautsi* the state was promoting the dominant religion and parents complained. Yet, underlying both cases are questions about the nature, meaning, and impact of religious symbolism. The difference in treatment of the impact of religious symbols on students in the two cases is striking. If these were the only two cases showing this kind of disparity one might wonder if *Dahlab* was limited to its very specific facts, but *Dahlab* is not the only case where a religious minority lost in a situation involving religious symbolism.

In *Kurtulmus v Turkey*,[25] a university professor was penalized for wearing a headscarf. Given that a university professor was involved, the case clearly did not involve young children. Yet again the state system, in this case Turkey, upheld the discipline. The professor brought the case to the ECHR under Article 9 and also under Article 8 dealing with the right to respect private life and Article 10 dealing with freedom of expression. The ECHR held that the professor did not have a valid claim. The ECHR held that when the relationship between the nation state and religion is at issue the nation state's role warrants a strong "margin of appreciation" and "special weight," that is, significant deference. Ironically, given the outcome in *Lautsi*, the ECHR said that wearing the headscarf could impact the rights of others and that because the Turkish civil service laws were neutral and promoted the secularism of the civil service, the implementation of the rule must be left to the national civil service. This raises the question of what exactly "neutrality" is in the law and religion context, as discussed in Chapter 1.

The *Dahlab* and *Kurtulmus* situations are not just limited to teachers. In several cases the ECHR came to similar decisions in cases involving students. This is where the differential treatment of religious symbols in *Lautsi* and the headcovering cases becomes most stark and most strained. It is certainly possible to argue that perhaps the context of teachers is a special exception because they are nation-state employees and therefore represent the state (there are numerous other ECHR decisions involving nonacademic nation-state employees), but the following cases, like *Lautsi*, involved impacts on students and student rights.

---

[25]   ECHR, January 24, 2006.

GOVERNMENT SUPPORT FOR RELIGION: PUBLIC EDUCATION 75

In *Leyla Sahin v Turkey*,[26] a Muslim medical student at the University of Istanbul wore a hijab because she believed it was her religious duty to do so. There was no question that she was a devout Muslim and that this was her sincere religious practice. In 1998 a rule came into effect that prohibited wearing a hijab in class or during exams. This rule forced her into an impossible position, so she left Turkey to pursue her studies elsewhere. She brought a claim under Article 9 of the European Convention of Human Rights and the claim reached the ECHR. The Grand Chamber of the ECHR found no violation of Article 9. In doing so the ECHR relied on deference to the nation state and explained that the Turkish Constitutional Court had found that wearing a hijab in public universities was a violation of the Turkish Constitution at that time. The ECHR found that she would have been aware of this and should have known a no-hijab rule might be possible at a public university. The ECHR went further and found that under Article 9 §2 the infringement of her religious practice could be considered "necessary in a democratic society," because wearing a hijab is often perceived as a compulsory religious duty which might have a negative impact on those who decided not to wear a hijab. Therefore, Turkey had the right to consider this impact.

This latter argument and the related deference to nation states is fascinating, given that there are many religious practices that are viewed as compulsory and many people who choose not to follow them. It is hard to understand why, without some sort of direct pressure from those who follow religious rules, there should be the equivalent of a heckler's veto for religious practices because nonbelievers might somehow be offended by religiousness. Yet, this argument is not limited to the *Leyla Sahin* case.

In *Köse and 93 others v Turkey*,[27] *Dogru v France*, and *Kervanci v France*,[28] students attending public secondary schools were the ones denied the ability to wear a hijab. In *Singh v France*,[29] public school students were also denied the ability to wear a keski, which is a small turban ordinarily worn under a larger turban by Sikh males.

---

[26]   ECHR, November 10, 2005 (Grand Chamber).
[27]   ECHR, January 24, 2006.
[28]   ECHR, December 4, 2008 (the *Dogru* and *Kervanci* cases were decided in a combined decision).
[29]   ECHR, June 30, 2009 (this decision combines several cases including cases involving hijab and keski).

76 ADVANCED INTRODUCTION TO LAW AND RELIGION

In *Köse*, students at state-funded religious schools were prevented from wearing a hijab in the schools even though the schools were Muslim-affiliated. The reason for this was that Turkey precluded the wearing of hijabs in any state-funded school. The students and their parents argued that the rule violated their right to manifest their religion in violation of Article 9. They also argued that the prohibition violated Article 2 of Protocol number 1 of the Convention, which protects the right to education. The reason for the Article 2 claim was that the students had been enrolled in the schools believing that they would receive an education consistent with the families' religion and the prohibition on wearing hijabs violated the ability to receive such an education. The ECHR dismissed the claim, finding the prohibition to be neutral and applicable to all students at state-funded schools regardless of religion. To the extent that it interfered with the students' rights to manifest their religion, the ECHR explained that there was not even the appearance of a violation of Article 9 because of the provision's neutrality. As to the Article 2 claim, the ECHR explained that the prohibition was based on "clear principles" and "proportionate" to Turkey's goals of protecting the neutrality of secondary education, protecting the rights of others, and minimizing disorder.

Two years later in the *Dogru* and *Kervanci* cases, the ECHR addressed a similar situation. In these cases, the students were expelled from a public secondary school in France for repeatedly refusing to remove their hijabs in gym classes when asked to do so. Doing so would, of course, have violated their religious beliefs. The ECHR found no violation of Article 9 because the national authorities' decision to require the removal during physical education classes was reasonable as it promoted health and safety concerns that were within France's right to protect. Yet, the ECHR went further and found that the expulsions were not based on the religious convictions but rather on the students' refusal to comply with school rules. This part of the opinion is question-begging given that the refusal to follow the rules was based on the religious convictions.

The following year, in *Singh*, the ECHR again addressed an issue arising in French public schools. The case involved the expulsion of six students from public schools for refusing to remove their keski (in the case of Sikh boys) and their hijabs (in the case of Muslim girls). The families brought complaints under Article 9 for violating the students' rights to manifest their religion. The ECHR dismissed the complaints, finding no viola-

GOVERNMENT SUPPORT FOR RELIGION: PUBLIC EDUCATION   77

tion of Article 9. The ECHR explained that the prohibition on wearing religious headwear was "prescribed by law" for the legitimate goal of protecting public order and the rights and freedoms of others. In doing so, the ECHR explained that the nation state, in this case France, occupied the role of a neutral arbiter of the exercise of various religions in the public sphere. The punishment of expulsion, the ECHR held, was proportionate to the violation, and the students could attend correspondence schools.

If not for *Lautsi*, one might just assume that the ECHR has been consistent in its treatment of religious symbols in the schools. Whether one were to agree or disagree with the outcomes, at least they would be consistent. Yet, *Lautsi* throws a wrench into this argument. One argument that might restore consistency is that the ECHR has deferred to the nation state in all the cases involving religious symbolism in schools. Therefore, *Lautsi* is no different than the other cases, except that in the other cases the nation states were promoting secularism while in *Lautsi* the nation state was not. Yet, as numerous scholars have explained, if this is so the ECHR is simply reifying majoritarian biases that find their way into the laws of nation states. As these scholars suggest, it renders Article 9 a paper tiger in many circumstances and disadvantages the religious freedom of religious minorities or unpopular religions. Interestingly, this is quite similar to the situation in the US, albeit through very different analysis and concepts.

3.2.4   A note on other religious exercises in public schools

Another type of religious exercise in public schools which has raised legal questions is moment of silence laws. These laws are generally constitutional in the US and legal in most other countries where they arise. Moment of silence laws have only been an issue in the US when they are either passed in an attempt to promote school prayer,[30] or are used to discriminate against religious minorities or dissenters.[31] As a result, other than in these unusual situations, most moment of silence laws are constitutional in the US. Additionally, they rarely raise any legal questions in other countries that have them.

---

[30]   *Wallace v Jaffree*, 472 U.S. 38 (1985).
[31]   *Walter v West Virginia Bd. of Education*, 610 F.Supp. 1169 (S.D. W.Va. 1985).

4. Government support for religion: public property

4.1 Public property

A number of issues can arise when public property is used for religious purposes. In some systems such use is not controversial, but in a number of systems religious symbolism on public property poses problems. Three main issues arise: first, the display of religious symbols on public property; second, the use of public property by religious groups, often referred to in the US as "equal access"; finally, the granting of public property to religious entities without compensation or with compensation below market value, or granting public property through favoritism toward religious groups.

4.1.1 Religious symbols on public property

This section addresses religious symbols on public property. It is limited to the display of religious symbols on government-owned property and does not address the grant of government property to religious entities, which is addressed in section 4.1.3. Nor does this section address religious symbols on private property. Finally, this section will focus mostly on the US, which has had numerous cases addressing this issue and raises some unique questions that also happen to shed light on the approaches of some other legal systems. Obviously, in many countries the government is free to display religious symbols while in some countries such displays are completely banned. In the US, however, the question is more nuanced and there are many cases addressing the issue which provide a variety of perspectives. At the outset it is important to note that the US Supreme

Court's recent decision in *Kennedy v Bremerton School District*[1] has called into question some of the precedent discussed below. However, because the *Kennedy* decision did not even cite the *McCreary County* decision discussed below and mischaracterized several other decisions also discussed, it remains to be seen what impact it might have on religious symbolism cases in the US. Regardless, the below cases provide a variety of approaches to the question; approaches that are reflected in other legal systems in addition to the United States.

Religious objects and religious symbolism generally do not lend themselves well to analysis under any legal test.[2] When a court evaluates a case involving religious objects it must subject those objects to the prevailing legal rules, norms, and analysis. It thus makes them legal subjects. This creates interpretive problems because of the potentially varied symbolic meaning of many religious objects and the various messages these objects can hold for various groups. It also raises questions regarding the nature of religious objects, since many symbolism cases involve objects that courts suggest exude varying levels of religiosity depending on their context, and which some critics suggest may or may not be perceived as religious depending on the perceiver's interpretive presumptions.

Thus, religious symbolism cases raise questions that implicate semiotics and hermeneutics. The symbolic meaning of the objects must be determined and analyzed within an interpretive framework where judges' preconceptions interact with the objects being interpreted. Unfortunately, the semiotic and hermeneutic concerns have often been addressed by courts in a reflexive way. This has led to a general failure to adequately explore the power of religious objects and a strong tendency to characterize them in a manner that reinforces a secularized, yet majoritarian, view of religion in public life. Ironically, the United States Supreme Court has led the way in creating this interpretive morass. As will be seen, the Court's recent cases do little to solve this problem, and may create additional questions.

---

[1]   ___ U.S. ___ (2022).

[2]   Frank S. Ravitch, *Religious Objects as Legal Subjects*, 40 WAKE FOREST LAW REVIEW 1011 (2005); *see also*, FRANK S. RAVITCH, MASTERS OF ILLUSION: THE SUPREME COURT AND THE RELIGION CLAUSES at 113–41 (NYU Press 2007).

80 ADVANCED INTRODUCTION TO LAW AND RELIGION

Religious objects are powerful representations that may connect to deeply held beliefs. For believers they may be symbols of, and conduits to, transcendent and very real truths. This may have an impact on how these objects are perceived by nonbelievers who are aware of the power the objects hold for believers. For others, these objects may retain some of the power they have for believers, or may simply be things to look at.

In one of the US Supreme Court's first cases addressing religious symbols on public property, *Lynch v Donnelly*,[3] the Court described a nativity scene as follows: "The creche, like a painting is passive; admittedly it is a reminder of the origins of Christmas. Even the traditional, purely secular displays extant at Christmas, with or without a creche, would inevitably recall the religious nature of the holiday."[4]

Putting aside for the moment the highly questionable assertions that a painting is "passive" and that any Christmas display can be "purely secular," the idea that a creche is "passive" is simply out of touch with well-accepted theological thought regarding religious symbols. Interestingly, Justice Rehnquist writing for the plurality in *Van Orden v Perry* (discussed below) referred to the Ten Commandments monument involved in that case as "passive," both before and after acknowledging its religious significance.

Several commentators have suggested that Justice Burger's description of the holiday display in *Lynch*, which included the creche, was the result of a reflexive application of his and the other Justices' preconceptions regarding these objects. These preconceptions, the argument goes, were both highly secularized and Christocentric. This seems a valid critique.

Any legal approach to religious objects should account for the fact that they are not just passive "things" but rather powerful conduits for religious meaning and cultural meaning, at least for believers. The theologian Paul Tillich characterized religious symbols as pointing beyond themselves to important religious meaning, while simultaneously participating "in the reality to which [they] point."[5] More specifically, in the context of a broader discussion of religious symbols, Tillich wrote: "Religious

---

[3]   465 U.S. 668 (1984).
[4]   *Id.* at 685.
[5]   PAUL TILLICH, SYSTEMATIC THEOLOGY (1951).

GOVERNMENT SUPPORT FOR RELIGION: PUBLIC PROPERTY   81

symbols are double-edged. They are directed toward the infinite which they symbolize and toward the finite through which they symbolize it. They force the infinite down to finitude and the finite up to infinity. They open the divine for the human and the human for the divine."[6]

Far from being the passive "things" depicted by the Court, religious symbols, including objects, can point to transcendental truth and are constitutive for the believer.

Yet, relying on the supposed passivity of the creche as well as a claimed tradition of displaying religious symbols on public property, the *Lynch* majority upheld the display of the creche as part of a broader Christmas display. The Court noted the long history of various forms of government interaction with religion, such as legislative chaplains. It acknowledged the religious meaning of the creche yet held that holiday displays are part of a long tradition connected to the winter holiday season and that Christmas has a secular aspect in addition to its religious aspects. The Court focused heavily on the importance of the broader context of the display, which included "a Santa Claus house, reindeer pulling a sleigh, candy-striped poles, a Christmas tree, carolers, cutout figures" of a "clown, an elephant, and a teddy bear, hundreds of colored lights, [and] a large banner that [read] 'Seasons Greetings'." It also noted the display's connection to the secular/commercial aspects of the holiday. In this context the display as a whole represented the secular aspects of Christmas. Thus, while the creche is a religious symbol, it did not foster a government establishment of religion in the context of the broader display and the holiday season, because that context demonstrated both a secular purpose and a primary effect that neither advanced nor inhibited religion under the then prevailing legal test.

In a concurring opinion, Justice O'Connor introduced the "endorsement test." While commentators have questioned Justice O'Connor's application of that test in *Lynch*, where she argued the creche did not violate the test, the test itself became highly influential, especially in cases involving government-supported or endorsed religious symbols. The test asks whether a reasonable observer familiar with the context and history of a government display would believe that the display creates insiders or outsiders along religious lines.

---

[6]   *Id.* at 240.

82   ADVANCED INTRODUCTION TO LAW AND RELIGION

In *County of Allegheny v American Civil Liberties Union*,[7] the Court again addressed a creche display. The case also involved the display of a menorah and a Christmas tree. The Court's analysis of the creche utilized the endorsement approach set forth by Justice O'Connor in *Lynch*. As in *Lynch*, the physical context of the creche display was central to the Court's decision. The creche was owned by the Holy Name Society, a Roman Catholic organization, and was located on the Grand Staircase of the county courthouse. It was not surrounded by sundry plastic figures and other "secular" symbols of the "holiday season," as had been the creche in *Lynch*. There was a sign denoting that the creche was donated by the Holy Name Society and there were also two small evergreen trees decorated with a red bow, but these basically blended into the manger scene depicted in the creche.

The different displays in the case led to different members of the Court being in the majority depending on the display. The majority held that the display of the creche violated the Establishment Clause because, unlike the creche in *Lynch*, the creche in the Allegheny County courthouse sent a message endorsing Christianity, and "nothing in the creche's setting detract[ed] from that message." Government may "acknowledge Christmas as a cultural phenomenon," but may not celebrate it as a "Christian holy day." The creche, which has an obvious religious message, is a celebration of the religious aspects of the holiday. Interestingly, *Lynch* and *Allegheny* together stand for the proposition that a patently religious symbol can somehow become adequately secularized if part of a larger holiday display celebrating the "secular aspects" of Christmas. The Court doesn't hold that the creche loses its religious nature based on its context, but rather that in some contexts its religious message is appropriately secularized such that government may display it.

The *Allegheny* decision also addressed the placement of a menorah outside the city-county building. The menorah was owned by Chabad-Lubavich, a Hasidic Jewish group, and was placed near a large Christmas tree and a sign saluting liberty. The Court acknowledged the religious nature and history of the menorah and the holiday of Chanukah, to which the menorah is related. Yet, the Court held that the context of the menorah—situated near the Christmas tree and sign saluting liberty—did not endorse Judaism or religion generally. Rather, the Court held that

---

[7]   492 U.S. 573 (1989).

GOVERNMENT SUPPORT FOR RELIGION: PUBLIC PROPERTY   83

the display sent a message recognizing religious pluralism and cultural diversity. The Court viewed the display as representing the winter holiday season rather than a specific religion or holiday.

Even though the majority opinion contained a rather detailed discussion of the theological and historical relevance of the menorah, the Court's approach demonstrates that there is an important difference between explaining the history of a religious object, or even discussing its role in ritual or theology, and carefully considering what an object's theological or ritualistic role says about the object. Justices Brennan captured this concern in his dissent, joined by Justices Marshall and Stevens. He agreed with the majority that Chanukah and the menorah are religious but disagreed that the context of the display could adequately secularize the menorah. He explained that, like the creche, the menorah is purely a religious object. Justice Brennan was concerned, as he was in *Lynch*, that the Court's decision would offend both believers and nonbelievers by minimizing the religious meaning of the object involved and by minimizing the impact these displays have on religious outsiders and nonbelievers.

In *ACLU v McCreary County*,[8] the Court explained the application of the purpose aspects of the endorsement test and the *Lemon* test to religious symbols on public property in the clearest and most detailed manner to date at that time. In *McCreary County* the Court held that Ten Commandments displays in two separate county courthouses were unconstitutional. The Court relied on the secular purpose prong of the *Lemon* and endorsement tests. The history of the displays in question played a significant role in the Court's analysis. Each of the displays originally consisted of a framed copy of the Ten Commandments taken from the King James version of the bible. The courthouse displays were readily visible to those using the courthouse. In response to a lawsuit aimed at forcing the counties to remove the displays, the counties modified the displays to include a variety of other documents, including "an excerpt from the Declaration of Independence [...] the Preamble to the Kentucky constitution [...] the national motto of 'In God We Trust' [...] [and] a page from the Congressional Record" declaring 1983 the year of the Bible. Each of the documents mentioned G-d and some documents were edited to include only the religious references contained in them. The district court

---

[8]   545 U.S. 844 (2005).

84 ADVANCED INTRODUCTION TO LAW AND RELIGION

granted the plaintiffs' request for a preliminary injunction despite these modifications to the displays.

In response the counties posted a third configuration of the displays that included fuller versions of some of the same documents contained in the second configuration, but also included some additional documents that did not reference G-d. The new displays also included a "prefatory document" that claimed the displays contained "documents that played a significant role in the foundation of our system of law and government." This document suggested that the Ten Commandments influenced the Declaration of Independence but made no attempt to connect the Ten Commandments to the other items in the display. This unsubstantiated connection was highly relevant to the Court of Appeals and also played a role in the Supreme Court's decision.

The majority opinion was authored by Justice Souter. The opinion focused heavily on the history of the display and the lack of a secular purpose evinced by that history. The Court's analysis begins with a quote from *Stone v Graham*,[9] discussed above in section 3.2.3, recognizing that the Ten Commandments "are undeniably a sacred text in the Jewish and Christian faiths." From there the Court moved into its secular purpose analysis, explaining that the *Stone* court found the religious nature of the Ten Commandments relevant in determining that there was no secular purpose. The Court's secular purpose analysis utilizes the *Lemon* test, but also uses the endorsement test. As for *Lemon*, the Court explained that the purpose analysis in that test is meant to assure government neutrality between religions "and between religion and nonreligion." Regarding the endorsement test, the Court explained that when government favors religion or a particular religion it sends a message to nonadherents that they are outsiders, not full members of the political community, and an accompanying message to adherents that they are insiders, favored members of the political community.

The majority rejected the counties' invitation to overturn or minimize the secular purpose test. Explaining why analysis of secular purpose is possible and not simply an exercise in getting into government actors' heads, Justice Souter wrote for the majority: "The eyes that look to purpose belong to an 'objective observer,' one who takes account of the traditional

---

[9]   449 U.S. 39 (1980) (per curium).

GOVERNMENT SUPPORT FOR RELIGION: PUBLIC PROPERTY   85

external signs that show up in the 'text, legislative history, and implementation of the statute,' or comparable official act."[10]

According to the Court, if an objective observer would perceive the predominant purpose behind a government action as religious, the government is "taking religious sides." In determining what an objective observer would perceive, the history and context of the display—of which the observer is presumed to be aware—are quite important.

The Court recognized that the *Stone* court had found the Commandments to be an "instrument of religion," and that this was decisive under the facts in that case. Still, the Court held that there is no per se rule against displaying the Ten Commandments under all circumstances.

Justice Souter, writing for the majority, points out that the text of the Commandments is a powerful indication of their religious nature and the likely religious purpose in displaying them. The majority opinion explains that where the text is absent it is less likely that an observer will perceive the depiction of tablets and the like as religious, and conversely when the text is present "the insistence of the religious message is hard to avoid" absent a context that suggests "a message going beyond an excuse to promote [a] religious point of view."

As a result, when the government places the text of the commandments "alone in public view"—as the counties did in the first of the three displays—the religious purpose is obvious. Moreover, surrounding the text with other historical documents, whose main connection is that they contain religious references, would only make a reasonable observer more likely to perceive a religious purpose.

The counties' third display, which included a number of secular documents and the text of the Ten Commandments, was ostensibly intended to represent the foundations of American law. The Court recognized that in a vacuum such a display might have a secular purpose, but in light of the history of the courthouse displays and the odd choices of historical documents—that is, including the Magna Carta and Declaration of Independence but not the Constitution or the Fourteenth Amendment—the displays could not survive secular purpose analysis. The Court found

---

[10]   *McCreary County*, 545 U.S. at 862.

86 ADVANCED INTRODUCTION TO LAW AND RELIGION

especially odd attempts to link the Ten Commandments, with their divine origin, and the Declaration of Independence, which derives governmental power from the people. Moreover, the Court noted the sectarian religious dedication ceremonies for each display.

The Court held that neutrality, although an elusive and variable concept, is an important focus of the religion clauses because the framers were concerned about the civic divisiveness that can be caused when the government takes sides in religious debates. This militates against the constitutionality of government displays that evince a religious purpose. The Court rejected the dissenting opinions' use of strict originalism because there are historical arguments that support both sides. Additionally, given the long line of precedent recognizing neutrality as a guiding principle, the Court did not find the dissent's reading of history persuasive.

Justice O'Connor, who joined the majority, filed a notable concurring opinion. She argued that given the religious divisiveness in nations without some level of separation, and given the success of the American experiment with separation—both for religion and society more generally—it makes little sense to reject core Establishment Clause principles and allow the government to favor one religion or set of religions over others or over nonreligion. She cited to the American tradition of religious voluntarism and wrote that when government endorses one religious tradition or another it can distort the marketplace of ideas and foster divisiveness.

Van Orden v Perry,[11] decided the same day as *McCreary County*, may seem at first glance to conflict with *McCreary County*. *Van Orden* is a split decision. Justice Rehnquist wrote the opinion for a plurality of Justices. Significantly, there are four Justices in the plurality and four dissenting Justices. Thus, Justice Breyer's opinion concurring in the judgment became the key opinion. When the US Supreme Court splits 4-1-4, the opinion that is most narrow and which joined the plurality to create a majority outcome often becomes the key opinion. In *Van Orden* this is Justice Breyer's opinion. Before addressing Justice Breyer's concurrence, however, it is useful to discuss the facts and the plurality opinion.

The case involved the display of a Ten Commandments monument on the ground between the Texas state capitol building and the state supreme

---

[11]   545 U.S. 677 (2005) (plurality opinion).

GOVERNMENT SUPPORT FOR RELIGION: PUBLIC PROPERTY   87

court building. The monument was one of several monuments scattered around the grounds of the capitol. Its location did not call any special attention to it. The monument was donated in 1961 by the Fraternal Order of Eagles and the Eagles paid the cost of erecting it. There was little evidence of the legislative intent behind accepting the monument and there was no evidence of the sort of religiously motivated purpose or dedication ceremony evident in *McCreary County*.

The plurality opinion begins by asserting that the Establishment Clause has a dual nature. It recognizes "the strong role played by religion and religious traditions throughout our nation's history" and at the same time it recognizes that "governmental intervention in religious matters can itself endanger religious freedom." The plurality applies analysis quite similar to that applied in *Lynch*; it does not apply either the *Lemon* or endorsement test. Thus, the plurality focuses on the "unbroken history of official acknowledgments by all three branches of government of the role of religion in American life" as asserted in *Lynch*. The opinion then recites several historical examples supporting this unbroken history and cites cases such as *Marsh v Chambers*,[12] which upheld legislative prayer because of its long history in the United States, and *Lynch* in combination with dicta from other cases. This is followed by discussion of the religious monuments and sculptures adorning federal buildings in the District of Columbia, including the Supreme Court. All of this is used as evidence that the Ten Commandments can have a secular meaning as well as a religious meaning, namely, the decalogue's historical role in American law and culture. Significantly, this seems to conflict with the Court's earlier holding in *Stone*, but the plurality distinguishes *Stone*, arguing that *Stone* involved the public schools where heightened Establishment Clause analysis has generally been applied.

The plurality opinion repeats the questionable argument from *Lynch* that religious objects can be "passive." Moreover, the plurality suggests that monuments such as the one in Texas can have "a dual significance, partaking of both religion and government." The argument seems to be that so long as the monument "partakes" of an appropriate secular "significance," the religious "significance," while still there, is somehow sterilized for Establishment Clause purposes. This approach has found recent support in the *American Humanist* case discussed below.

---

[12]   483 U.S. 783 (1983).

88 ADVANCED INTRODUCTION TO LAW AND RELIGION

As mentioned above, Justice Breyer's opinion is key to understanding the outcome in *Van Orden*. Several themes emerge in Justice Breyer's concurrence. First, Justice Breyer views the situation in *Van Orden* as a "borderline" case to which no legal test can be appropriately applied. A borderline case leaves only the "exercise of legal judgement" for determining the outcome. Justice Breyer stresses, however, that such legal judgment is not a personal judgment: "Rather […] it must reflect and remain faithful to the underlying purposes of the clauses, and it must take account of context and consequences measured in light of those purposes." Second, Justice Breyer, like the plurality, writes that the purpose of the Establishment Clause is maintaining some level of separation between church and state while avoiding hostility to religion, although it seems clear that Justice Breyer weighs these factors differently than the plurality. Third, Justice Breyer asserts that avoiding religious divisiveness is a major goal of the Establishment Clause, but this can cut both ways. Therefore, the type of religious purpose evidenced in *McCreary County* is unconstitutional, but so would be attempts by the "government to purge from the public sphere all that in any way partakes of the religious." Fourth, Justice Breyer argues that longstanding religious displays do not generally raise the same Establishment Clause concerns as new attempts to display religious objects, because the longstanding displays are less likely to be divisive, assuming their context and purpose adequately secularizes them. This seems to be an attempt to protect most longstanding government displays that include religious themes against Establishment Clause challenge. Justice Breyer rejects most of the plurality's reasoning and seems to carve out a narrow group of cases involving longstanding religious monuments or displays whose physical and historical context make them appear less divisive than they might appear in other historical or physical settings.

The law relating to public display of religious objects by government entities seemed a bit unclear after *McCreary County* and *Van Orden*, but some things were quite clear. For example, if a display does not have a secular purpose it is unconstitutional, because a majority of the Court in *McCreary County* held that without a secular purpose a display is unconstitutional. If there is an adequate secular purpose the *Van Orden* plurality would apply a tradition approach, but it is unclear whether Justice Breyer would do so except in "borderline" cases, and of course, Justice Breyer did not agree with the bulk of the plurality opinion. The key after these cases is that questions about the physical and historical context of a given display were relevant in religious symbolism cases.

GOVERNMENT SUPPORT FOR RELIGION: PUBLIC PROPERTY   89

In *American Legion v American Humanist Association*,[13] decided 14 years later, the Court seemed to follow Justice Breyer's approach in a case involving a World War I monument.

In *American Humanist Association*, a World War I war memorial in the form of a Latin cross had come over time to be located on public land in the middle of a busy traffic circle in Maryland. Its location in the middle of the traffic circle was a result of increased population and development. The American Humanist Association challenged the cross because it was prominently located on public land and was also the location for religious events on some occasions. The American Legion, which is an association for war veterans, argued that because the Latin cross is a longstanding war memorial for World War I veterans and the cross was often used in memorials for soldiers in World War I, it would be hostile to religion to move the cross or cut its arms off to make it into the shape of a stelae, as the American Humanist Association had proposed.

Making the case even more interesting, a variety of non-Christian war veteran groups, including the Jewish War Veterans Association, argued in amicus briefs that the Latin cross is not an appropriate memorial for non-Christian war veterans. This argument was reflected in Justice Ginsburg's strong dissenting opinion.

The majority held that the war memorial was constitutional because it had a long and unbroken history of serving as a war memorial and that while using a Latin cross as a war memorial today could be problematic, it was viewed as acceptable, and was somewhat common, after World War I. The Court relied on the history of World War I and the specific war memorial in question to find that the memorial did not violate the Establishment Clause. The Court held it would be hostile to religion to remove or alter the memorial, given its history. The Court also made clear that while a Latin cross is today seen as a sectarian symbol, at the time the memorial was created it was viewed as appropriate. Justice Ginsburg's dissent strongly refutes this point with a great deal of evidence, but the majority's response is that the memorial needs to be viewed in its historical and traditional context—that is, as it would have been viewed then—and not from today's perspective. Justice Ginsburg replied that even then

---

[13]   588 U.S. ___ (2019).

90 ADVANCED INTRODUCTION TO LAW AND RELIGION

it would have been viewed as inappropriate by the many non-Christians who died fighting for the US in World War I.

In the end, the majority essentially carved out an exception for long-standing war memorials and acknowledged that if a cross was placed by government on public property today, the result might be different. The majority relied on the unique context of the display as a war memorial and on the history and tradition approach reflected in *Lynch* and *Van Orden*. In a sign of things to come, Justices Gorsuch, Kavanaugh, and Thomas each filed concurring opinions calling for the rejection of the *Lemon* and endorsement approaches while Justices Breyer and Kagan filed concurring opinions arguing that this case does not alter those tests in situations where they may be relevant. The latter concurring opinions explained that a World War I war memorial is a unique—or, as Justice Breyer suggested in *Van Orden*, perhaps a borderline—situation because of the age and history of the war memorial and the hostility to religion that would be demonstrated by moving or altering the war memorial. In the end the outcome of the case was decided by a 7–2 majority, but the majority opinion was more limited than some of the concurrences would have liked.

The concurrences that argued for overturning *Lemon* and the endorsement test would find their way into the majority in the *Kennedy* case decided in 2022 and mentioned throughout this chapter. After *Kennedy* it is unclear what the prevailing rule will be in religious symbolism cases. It seems that both the *Lemon* and endorsement tests are now gone and that a significantly expanded version of the *American Humanist Association* approach will apply, but the *Kennedy* case involved a context different from that of public displays of religious symbols, and the *Kennedy* majority, while citing *Van Orden* and *American Humanist Association*, failed to even mention *McCreary County* and several other opinions relevant in the religious symbolism context. This could just be a reflection of the questionable analysis that is a hallmark of the *Kennedy* opinion,[14] or it

---

[14] After all, an American lawyer who failed to cite a relevant opinion damaging to their case could be sanctioned, and given the fact that *Kennedy* relies heavily on cases like *Van Orden* and *American Humanist Association* in its rejection of the *Lemon* and endorsement tests in the context of a public school football coach praying on the 50-yard line after games, *McCreary County*—and its defense of the *Lemon* and endorsement purpose analysis—is obviously as relevant as the other religious symbolism cases cited by the

could mean that *McCreary County* is still good law in religious symbolism cases. The likelihood is that the latter is not the case, but until the Court clarifies itself on this question it makes sense to give the Court the benefit of the doubt given that the alternative is that the *Kennedy* majority opinion did not just reject 50 years of precedent—which seems clear—but did so in an intellectually dishonest manner.

There are other issues that have arisen in the religious symbolism context, such as the display of private religious symbols in a public forum open to free speech, or when the government sells land on which a religious symbol is displayed. The first of these questions will be addressed in section 4.1.2 below and the second, in the context of the *Sunigawa City* cases from Japan, in section 4.1.3 below.

4.1.2   Access to public property by religious groups

Access to public property by religious groups—often referred to as "equal access"—is not a problematic issue in many systems. Religious groups can access public property under a variety of circumstances, but the circumstances and the underlying bases for this access can vary by system. Moreover, in some systems access by some or all religious groups to public property is prohibited, or, as is the case in the United States, access is dependent on whether the public property is open to free speech more generally.

Given the vast array of different systems for access to public property, it is tempting to end the discussion here. There have been numerous cases in the US on the subject, however, and questions have arisen in some other countries as well. The issue in some countries outside of the US is whether unrecognized religions are able to access public property for meetings, protests, and similar. The question of recognized versus unrecognized religions was addressed a bit in Chapters 1 and 2, but as a reminder, in many countries—especially in Europe—some religions are recognized by the state while others are not. This recognition can take many forms and the benefits of state recognition vary from minor benefits to outright favoritism.

Kennedy majority and would need to be discussed even if only to distinguish or overturn it.

92   ADVANCED INTRODUCTION TO LAW AND RELIGION

A good example of the minor benefit approach comes from outside Europe. In Japan, organizations that register under the Religious Juridical Persons Act (宗教法人法, *Shuukyou Hojin Hou*) can gain limited benefits and other protections, but religions that choose not to register still have the full protection of all other laws, including the Japanese Constitution. Moreover, it is generally up to religious groups whether they want to register under the Act. By contrast, several countries in Europe have official state religions and several other "recognized religions" that receive much greater benefits than unrecognized religions, and several other countries have no official religion but do recognize certain religions for benefits.

Thus, in Japan any limitation on a religious group accessing public property such as a community center for a meeting would be based on the constitutional separation of politics and religion, and assuming no government favoritism toward a given religion, access would simply be based on the general community access policies. Moreover, religious groups would have the same free speech rights and restrictions as other groups. Yet, in some European countries, only "recognized religions" would have a right to access public property. Of course, in many other European countries access to public property for meetings, protests, and so on is not limited to "recognized religion" and in these countries recognition is more about tax benefits and financial subsidies than it is about access to public buildings or other property, such as parks, on the same terms as other groups.

In the US this issue is complex but has a clear-cut answer. Basically, in the US there is no such thing as a recognized religion. The main question about access to public property is based on free speech rights and the nature of the property. The latter helps determine the former.

In the US, public property can be divided into three rough categories relating to private speech. First is the public forum. Public forums are open to private speech generally and the government cannot engage in discrimination based on the content or viewpoint of that speech. Examples of public forums are public parks, sidewalks, and specified "free speech" areas on other public property. Second is the "limited" or "designated" public forum. These are public forums limited to a specific time and/or location, and/or limited to a designated group. The government also cannot discriminate based on content or viewpoint in a limited or designated public forum. Examples of limited public forums are school

GOVERNMENT SUPPORT FOR RELIGION: PUBLIC PROPERTY 93

buildings open to noncurriculum-related groups before or after school hours. An example of a designated public forum could be a bulletin board limited to student use. As a practical matter, the terms "limited public forum" and "designated public forum" are often used interchangeably by US courts.

When it comes to access to government property by religious groups, most of the fights have been over whether a school or other municipal or state building has been opened to private speech at certain times and whether government concerns about establishment of religion can justify excluding religious groups from these limited public forums. The answer from the US Supreme Court has been uniform. If the government creates a limited or designated public forum it cannot exclude religious groups from that forum without violating the Free Speech Clause of the First Amendment to the United States Constitution. Excluding a religious group from an otherwise open forum would be content or viewpoint discrimination.

The only way the government can engage in content or viewpoint discrimination would be if it can meet strict scrutiny. That is, the government would need to show that denying access serves a compelling governmental interest and that doing so is the least restrictive means of serving that interest. In a series of cases, school districts or other government entities argued that religious groups were excluded from a public forum or limited public forum because of concerns that allowing the group access would violate the Establishment Clause of the First Amendment to the United States Constitution. The government entities have lost every one of these cases because the Court has held that private speech in a public forum cannot be attributed to the government and is not state action. Therefore, the Establishment Clause concern cannot serve as a compelling interest.

These cases have involved a range of issues, from a hate group's placement of a cross in a public forum open to free speech generally at a state capitol to access by religious groups or religious student clubs to public schools before or after classes. These public schools had opened their property to noncurriculum-related groups during those times. If the school was not open to outside or noncurriculum-related student groups there would be no duty to allow a religious group access, because there is no public or limited public forum for free speech. This is important because giving religious groups preferential access to public property could violate the

94 ADVANCED INTRODUCTION TO LAW AND RELIGION

Establishment Clause. Notice the difference in the situations. In an "equal access" situation the government is excluding a religious group from a public or limited public forum which would violate the Free Speech Clause, while in the latter situation the government is giving preferred access to a public or limited public forum (or to government property that is not a public or limited public forum) to a religious group which could violate the Establishment Clause.

4.1.3 Grants of public property to religious entities

For the purposes of this subsection, the issue of government grants of public property to religious entities is limited to grants of real property. Chapter 5 addresses government grants of funding and other resources. Systems around the world range from those in which the grant of public property to religious institutions is common, or at the very least not problematic, to those where it is absolutely prohibited. One of the most interesting systems is the Japanese system, discussed in more depth below. As will be seen, in Japan the government is constitutionally prohibited from giving public property to religious entities without compensation, but can recognize religious property as a Cultural Heritage Site.

In the US the government is constitutionally prohibited from giving real property to religious entities without fair compensation, but issues have arisen about who might have standing to sue if the federal government gave property to a religious entity.[15] In Europe a variety of systems exist, ranging from permissive grants of public land to religious entities to absolute prohibition of grants of public land to religious entities. The Japanese system captures some of the most common approaches to this issue among democratic systems. It will be used as an example to address the range of possibilities because the general constitutional parameters in the Japanese system have been explained in previous sections and chapters, so readers will have background on the underlying constitutional limitations. Moreover, the Japanese system also addresses questions about historical sites that still operate as functioning religious institutions.

---

[15] *Valley Forge Christian College v Americans United for Separation of Church and State*, 454 U.S. 464 (1982).

GOVERNMENT SUPPORT FOR RELIGION: PUBLIC PROPERTY   95

In the *Sunagawa Sorachibuto Shrine Case*,[16] the city of Sunagawa in Hokkaido gave a neighborhood religious association called the *Ujiko* the use of city-owned property as a Shinto shrine without requesting any compensation from the association. This was challenged by a resident of the city as violating the Constitution. The case eventually made its way to the Japanese Supreme Court, which considered the purpose and effect of the grant by considering how the situation would be viewed from the Japanese public's perspective.

The Japanese Supreme Court held that the city's actions violated both Article 20 and Article 89 of the Japanese Constitution and explained that the analysis under these Articles overlaps. The fact that the shrine was originally taken over by the city at the request of a local citizen who had donated the land (for tax reasons) did not change this analysis. The Court recognized the religious nature of Shintō shrines, and the problems raised by perceived government favoritism toward the shrine. In holding that the use of a government meeting building to house a religious shrine, especially without any compensation, would be viewed from the public's perspective as favoring Shintoism, the Court provided a more in-depth discussion of Article 89 itself than prior cases had done:

> Article 89 of the Constitution can be construed to prohibit the state's or local public entity's connection with religion in cases where its connection with religion in terms of appropriating public property for use, etc. is found to be beyond the limit that is deemed to be reasonable, in light of the social and cultural conditions of our country, in relation to the fundamental purpose of the system of securing [the] guarantee of freedom of religion.
>
> The act of the state or a local public entity to offer national or public land for use as a site for a religious facility without compensation should be, in general, deemed to constitute offering of a benefit to the religious organization, etc. which has established said religious facility, and it raises a conflict with Article 89 of the Constitution.[17]

---

[16]   64 SAIKO SAIBANSHO MINJI HANREISHU [MINSHU] no. 1 [Grand Bench 2010].

[17]   Quotes from these cases in this book are from the unpaginated official English translation of the cases. The Japanese versions are the official versions of the cases and are paginated.

96   ADVANCED INTRODUCTION TO LAW AND RELIGION

The Court also explained that context is very important when considering whether offering public land for use of a religious facility without compensation violates Article 89. In this regard, the Court explained:

> [I]t is appropriate to construe that judgment should be made comprehensively in light of socially accepted ideas, while taking into consideration various factors, including the nature of the religious facility in question, the circumstances where the land in question has been offered for the use as the site of the relevant facility without compensation, the manner of offering without compensation, and the public's evaluation of such practice.[18]

The Court held that the situation in the case violated these principles. It noted, however, that it would be inappropriate to require the mayor to remove the shrine immediately because it would make it very hard for the *Ujiko* group to carry out its religious activities, which would harm the religious freedom of members of the group. Remanding the case to see whether any "rational and realistic alternative means" other than total removal of the shrine was possible, the Court noted several possible alternatives, including a grant, transfer for compensation, or lease at fair market value. The Court itself seemed to favor a remedy that involved compensation or a lease at fair market value, but since it also mentioned a grant, it is not clear what would be required. In a subsequent decision a Petty Bench of the Court ultimately approved a lease at fair market value.[19]

In another judgment rendered the same day, but involving a different shrine in Sunagawa City,[20] the Court upheld a transfer by the municipal government to a neighborhood association of a Shinto shrine and the small parcel of land on which it sat. The transfer of the land and shrine had been challenged by municipal residents as a violation of Article 20(3) and Article 89. Interestingly, the Court noted that, given the religious nature of a Shinto shrine, the city might be viewed by the public to be favoring religion. The Court explained, however, that the land had originally belonged to the predecessor of the same neighborhood association,

---

[18]   *Id.*

[19]   *Sunagawa City II*, 66 SAIKO SAIBANSHO MINJI HANREISHU [MINSHU] no. 2 [1st Petty Bench 2012].

[20]   *Sunagawa City Failure to Administer Property Case*, 64 SAIKO SAIBANSHO MINJI HANREISHU [MINSHU] no. 1 (gyo-tsu No. 334) [Grand Bench 2010].

which had donated it to the city to build housing for public school teachers, which was no longer there. As a result, the land transfer to the association was viewed by the Court as a return of land given to the city for a specific purpose that was no longer being served. Under these facts the Court considered the transfer an acceptable way to avoid problems under Article 20 and Article 89 that would have existed had the city continued to own land used by the shrine free of charge. Thus, despite the seeming similarities, the facts of the case were decisively different from the facts in the *Sunagawa Sorachibuto Shrine* case.

In 2021 the Court addressed similar issues in the context of a religion other than Shintō for the first time, in a case from Okinawa involving a Confucian temple. The government of the city of Naha allowed the temple to build a new facility in a public park without paying any rent or fees. The Court held that this violated both Article 20 and Article 89. It followed the reasoning from the *Sunagawa Sorachibuto Shrine* case to hold that allowing the temple to build on and occupy the land in a public park without paying rent unconstitutionally promoted religion.[21] The court also distinguished the temple from historical religious sites that are able to be on public land without fees because of their historical nature and a longstanding presence at their location (the temple was built in the park in 2013).

These cases illustrate that the context and history of any land transfer given to a religious entity will be important to the analysis under Article 89 (and Article 20) of the Japanese Constitution. The Court will consider the issue from the perspective of whether the public would view the government as favoring religion, and the Court has not been afraid to find that a violation has occurred.

Of course, in most situations the role of the Japanese Supreme Court is not as pronounced as that of the US Supreme Court, and the Japanese system in many ways resembles the German and French systems. Thus, many issues are governed by the civil code or various property laws unless they raise constitutional issues. One question that has arisen in Japan, given its

---

[21] While some might argue that Confucianism is a philosophy, not a religion, the court held that the performance of rites at the temple had enough of a religious function to be covered under Article 20 and Article 89; however, it did so without specifically holding that Confucianism is a religion.

98 ADVANCED INTRODUCTION TO LAW AND RELIGION

long history and the many temples and shrines that remain active today in the same locations they have occupied for hundreds of years, is what happens when the land on which the temple or shrine sits has become part of a larger tract of public property in recent years. Another question that has arisen is what should and can be done for historical religious sites that are part of the cultural heritage of Japan.

The first question is referenced in the case from Okinawa above. If a long-standing religious location later becomes located on public land because of a change in the status of the land on which it is located, an exception can be made so that the religious entity need not pay the government a fee to stay in its historical location—for example, a public park or designated wilderness or protected area. This would only apply if the religious buildings were located on the property as a historical matter. Bear in mind that in Japan it is not uncommon that a temple or shrine may have been in the same location for more than 1,000 years, and the property was obviously not public during most of that time.

The second question is quite important in Japan, which has numerous historical sites—including many temples and shrines—that are connected to Japanese heritage. The Japanese government can designate historical sites as Tangible Cultural Property or Japan Heritage Sites. Tangible Cultural Property can be further broken down into National Treasures, Important Cultural Properties, and Registered Tangible Cultural Properties in order of importance. These properties can receive limited government financial support for their preservation and protection, such as conservation, major repairs, and disaster prevention, but that support does not go beyond protecting the structures or any art or statues that are themselves designated as Tangible Cultural Properties. Designation as a Tangible Cultural Property, especially as a National Treasure, may increase attention and tourism at the sites, which could indirectly benefit the religious sects that own the sites if they charge admission or sell things, but this is viewed as an indirect result of the categorization, and religious Tangible Cultural Property sites receive no more benefits than their nonreligious counterparts. This system has been found to be constitutional given its primary focus on preserving Japanese history and culture without regard to its religious connection or lack of religious connection.

The Japan Heritage Site designation helps protect the history of the sites and their connection to the local community. It does not grant any

GOVERNMENT SUPPORT FOR RELIGION: PUBLIC PROPERTY   99

funds for repair or maintenance. Nor does it provide funding for disaster prevention.

Thus, Japan has managed to prevent government transfer of public property without fair compensation while maintaining the flexibility to protect important historical sites without subsidizing religion qua religion. Naturally, the fact that an ancient temple or shrine may get funding to preserve or protect its structures and/or artifacts will be of help to the temple or shrine, but failure to provide that funding might lead to the loss or structural degradation of important historical sites. Moreover, religious sites are far from the only Tangible Cultural Property sites, and all receive the same sorts of historical preservation support.

4.2   Free speech and the public/private distinction

As explained above, questions about the nature of religious speech have arisen, especially in the US. The question is often whether the speech is public or private speech, and this question arises in a variety of contexts, from school prayer to religious symbolism on public property. In many systems private speech is highly protected even on public property. Yet questions arise as to whether private speech can be viewed as government speech in certain contexts. This issue is especially complex in the US—and may have gotten more confusing after the US Supreme Court's recent decision in *Kennedy*, which threw out decades of precedent and turned much of the analysis of what counts as private speech in the public school context on its head. The upside of the decision is that in some situations, the question may have become easier to resolve. The downside is that the resolution may now be highly formalistic, despite the complexity of the underlying issues, and may be harmful to religious minorities and nonbelievers. The latter concern arises because the US Supreme Court's new approach is likely to favor the most dominant and loud religions at the expense of everyone else. The *Kennedy* decision was addressed a bit in Chapter 3 but will be considered in more depth here.

As explained in Chapter 3, *Kennedy* overturned *Lemon v Kurtzman* and significantly called into question the endorsement test, although there are arguments that endorsement might survive in some contexts because the Court failed even to cite important cases using that test. The

100 ADVANCED INTRODUCTION TO LAW AND RELIGION

indirect coercion test likely survived the *Kennedy* decision, but the key to understanding *Kennedy* in the free speech context may have less to do with the law and more to do with the *Kennedy* majority's shocking mischaracterization of the facts in the case and the impact that may have on other decisions.

Prior to *Kennedy* the law was already relatively clear, but it remained complex and required a fact-specific analysis. Private religious speech is protected from content or viewpoint discrimination in a public forum or limited public forum unless the government can meet strict scrutiny when interfering with that speech. Moreover, unless the government is favoring the religious speech in a public or limited public forum, the Establishment Clause does not provide a compelling interest that would support government interference with private religious speech.

Some speech, however, is considered government speech, which is not subject to the free speech tests applicable to private speech in a public forum.[22] Government speech, however, may be more likely to violate the Establishment Clause. The analysis of whether speech is government speech under the Free Speech Clause and the question of whether that speech violates the Establishment Clause are fact-specific.

The *Kennedy* case falls at the nexus between private speech and government speech, but the Court so vastly mischaracterized the facts that it is hard to know how to deal with the situation as it actually was. The dissent includes pictures of some of the events that would normally have been central to the Court's analysis prior to *Kennedy* but which the majority outright ignores or severely mischaracterizes. This will leave lower courts to determine how to apply the case in circumstances similar to what actually happened in *Kennedy*, versus circumstances where the facts are actually as the *Kennedy* majority claimed they were and situations in between. It is important to note that courts often characterize facts in a manner that supports the holding in a case, but *Kennedy* goes far beyond that by ignoring almost every key fact in the record and mischaracterizing others. Reading the full record from the trial court in the case and then reading the majority opinion is like going through the looking glass.[23]

---

[22] *Pleasant Grove City v Summum*, 555 U.S. 460 (2009).

[23] Lewis Carroll, Alice's adventures in Wonderland (T. Y. Crowell & Co, 1893).

GOVERNMENT SUPPORT FOR RELIGION: PUBLIC PROPERTY   101

A summary of the actual facts of the case follows. The actual facts of the case as documented in the record and in the dissenting opinion with photographs of the events are that Kennedy, an assistant coach for a public high school football team and junior varsity head coach, kneeled and prayed after football games at the 50-yard line. For years he prayed with his own players and invited players and coaches from opposing teams and others to pray with him, in violation of school district policy. He also gave religiously themed speeches along with the prayer at the 50-yard line. Additionally, he prayed with students in the locker room, but that was a tradition that pre-dated his doing so and which was stopped once the school was informed about it (players could still pray without the coaches).

The school district informed Kennedy that he needed to stop involving students in the 50-yard-line prayers and could come back out to the field and pray on his own after his coaching duties for the day concluded. At first, he followed the school district's request, but he then had a change of heart; he began again to pray immediately after games and invited players and coaches from the opposing team to pray with him. He was warned again and announced to the media that he would pray at the 50-yard line at an upcoming game. After the media coverage the district began to receive threatening messages, letters, and emails. This led to a frenzy after a game where fans came down from the stands to pray with him, trampling students, school band members, and others. The district had to hire security for games after these events. School employees and administrators were threatened, the community became divided over the prayer, and it turned into a media spectacle. Kennedy continued to kneel and demonstratively pray at the 50-yard line immediately after games after being warned several times by the school district not to do so. The district offered to work with Kennedy on a compromise where he could come back to the field to pray after fulfilling his duties to the team, but he would only accept demonstrative prayer directly after the game.

Prior to his turning the prayer into a spectacle it might have been possible for him to quietly pray on his own at the 50-yard line shortly after games, but given all the attention he called to the prayer and the fact that he was a school employee wearing school logos and the like, the district was concerned about being viewed as endorsing the prayer and about his flauting school district rules and requests. After he ignored repeated warnings by the district, he was disciplined and not rehired. He then sued.

102 ADVANCED INTRODUCTION TO LAW AND RELIGION

The majority characterization of the facts is summed up in the first line of the opinion: "Joseph Kennedy lost his job as a high school football coach because he knelt at midfield after games to offer a quiet prayer of thanks." The majority states that Kennedy quietly prayed at the 50-yard line after games and, after being warned about student involvement in prayers, no longer prayed with students after games or in the locker room. The majority states that the district was worried about perceptions that Kennedy might be endorsing religion through demonstratively praying when students are around and thus targeted Kennedy because of his prayers. The majority suggests that it was the targeting of Kennedy's conduct due to the school district's Establishment Clause concerns that led to the media attention that eventually occurred. It also states that Kennedy was willing to work with the district on a compromise but that the district disciplined him for his religious speech.

If the facts were as the majority states it really would be an easy case, and there would have been no need to overturn *Lemon* or call the endorsement test into question. If a coach just went quietly to the 50-yard line after games, when people could engage in all types of speech, and said a quiet personal prayer, there would be little question that the speech is private. It would be likely that for that short period after games and before players and coaches went back to the locker room, the field became a limited public forum for coaches and players to talk about anything. Even if it were not a limited public forum, it would fall within the sort of protected speech government employees can have on government property.[24] Moreover, since no students would be involved, and the prayer would not be demonstrable (other than perhaps a bowed head) or loud, there would not likely be an Establishment Clause violation under any of the Establishment Clause tests at that time, whether the *Lemon* test, the endorsement test, or the indirect coercion test.

But those were not the facts. The facts suggest a public school employee not only praying with students, but praying with students who might feel coerced to pray or lose their position, or experience peer pressure. Moreover, that same employee turned his 50-yard-line prayer into a public spectacle that divided a community. It is clear that, prior to *Kennedy* and given the *Santa Fe v Doe* decision discussed in section 3.2.1,

---

[24]   *Garcetti v Ceballos*, 547 U.S. 410 (2005).

Kennedy's prayers would not have been considered private speech under the actual facts considering all the circumstances.

Even if Kennedy's prayers were somehow found to be private speech, all three Establishment Clause tests used in public school cases prior to *Kennedy* would likely have been violated under the actual facts of the case because of Kennedy's power over players, his proximity to indicia of the school, and his loud and divisive actions for which he sought attention from players and coaches from both teams in a given game and the media. The Establishment Clause concern would have served as a compelling interest for the discipline and the only remaining question would have been whether the discipline was the least restrictive means of achieving the compelling interest. It is this last issue that would have posed the biggest issue for the district under the then prevailing test if indeed Kennedy's speech was found to be private.

The question now is: After *Kennedy*, what will happen in future cases where courts find either that the speech is not private and/or that there was indirect coercion of students to participate in the prayer due to concerns about upsetting a coach that has power over their playing time and/or concerns about peer pressure? Also, would the endorsement test still apply in such a situation, given that the *Kennedy* majority did not discuss that test's key role in *Santa Fe v Doe* and did not even cite the *McCreary County* case discussed above? After *Kennedy* the answers are unclear.

4.3   Legislative prayer

Legislative prayer can involve prayer before, during, or after the meeting of any legislative body, whether national, state/prefectural, or local. The prayer may be delivered by a chaplain of some sort; by invited guests, including clergy; or by the legislators themselves. There are many different contexts in which this can occur. This section will focus on prayer at legislative sessions, including everything from national legislatures such as Congress to local legislative bodies such as city councils.

Globally, there are numerous systems for legislative prayer. They range from extremely permissive (or, in theocracies, mandated) to systems where legislative prayer is prohibited. At this point it should come as no

104 ADVANCED INTRODUCTION TO LAW AND RELIGION

shock that the country in which the issue has been most litigated is the United States, although there have been disagreements over the issue in other systems as well. As scholars in this field well know, not all systems see the need to settle these issues through litigation!

In the US, the litigation battle lines were drawn in a 1983 case called *Marsh v Chambers*.[25] However, disagreements in the US over legislative prayer are as old as the US itself. In *Marsh*, the Court upheld the practice of legislative prayer delivered by a chaplain in Nebraska's unicameral legislature. The Court majority did not apply the *Lemon* test, which was the primary test applicable at that time, because of the long, unbroken history of legislative prayer in the United States. In other words, legislative prayer is an exception to the then prevailing general rule of relatively strong separation. Yet, until 2014 it was generally thought that for legislative prayer to be constitutional, it had to be nonsectarian and non-proselytizing.[26]

In *Town of Greece v Galloway*,[27] the Supreme Court addressed a situation that had become somewhat common in municipalities around the country; namely, a town council had invited local clergy to come deliver an invocation before meetings. The clergy were invited by using the local phone book. The difference, however, as explained in great detail in Judge Calabrese's opinion for the Second Circuit Court of Appeals,[28] was that the town of Greece gerrymandered the selection so that, until discovery in the case, all the prayers delivered were Christian and often sectarian. Moreover, town council members regularly crossed themselves before the prayers and the prayer practice had not been longstanding in the town. There were many non-Christians in the town but because their population in the area was not large enough to support a house of worship in each local town, synagogues, mosques, and temples were located near the town of Greece but not in it (although there was a Buddhist temple in the town).

The key for present purposes is that the Court, over a strong dissent, held that this sort of legislative prayer need not be non-sectarian, and the town

---

[25] 463 U.S. 783 (1983).

[26] See, e.g., *County of Allegheny v American Civil Liberties Union*, 492 U.S. 573 (1989); *Wynne v Town of Great Falls*, 376 F.3d 292 (4th Cir. 2004).

[27] 572 U.S. 565 (2014).

[28] *Galloway v Town of Greece*, 681 F.3d 20 (2nd Cir. 2012).

GOVERNMENT SUPPORT FOR RELIGION: PUBLIC PROPERTY   105

need not invite clergy from outside the town in order for the prayer to be constitutional. The prayer, however, could still not be used to discriminate or to openly proselytize. Thus, today in the US, unless legislative prayer is used to intentionally discriminate or openly proselytize, it is constitutional even if it only represents a single religion. The *Galloway* court, like the *Marsh* court, relied heavily on the unbroken history of legislative prayer in the US.[29]

4.4   Ceremonial deism

Ceremonial deism is a term for things that represent civic religion. These are things that may involve religious imagery or language but have often been longstanding practices in a given nation. It is usually a practice that is generally nonsectarian but obviously has some religious aspect, such as the "In God We Trust" on US money.[30] The things that fall under this category are often excluded from general rules regarding government promotion of religion. The question of ceremonial deism is fraught for many reasons, not least of which is the fact that there is no coherent definition of what counts as ceremonial deism, at least in the US. Moreover, there are many arguments as to why ceremonial deism should or should not be subject to the same rules as other governmental religious expression. The many questions surrounding ceremonial deism are beyond the scope of this advanced introduction and would support an entirely separate volume(s) on civic religion.

---

[29]   As the dissent points out, however, the early Congresses sought to avoid what would have been viewed as sectarian prayer at that time in favor of nonsectarian (albeit pan-Protestant) prayer, and the tradition of prayer at local government meetings is less well known than state and national legislative prayer practices.

[30]   The singular reference to a deity would of course not be completely nonsectarian as it would exclude religions with multiple deities, no deity, or a deity with a specific name that does not fit under the more general reference.

5. Government support for religion: funding and tax exemptions

5.1 Funding

Government funding for religious use is at the same time one of the most straightforward and one of the most complex issues in law and religion, depending on the system involved. Funding issues arise most frequently in the context of government financial or other support for religious schools or religious education generally, but have also arisen in contexts such as funding which goes directly to houses of worship or to religious groups more generally.

In many systems the ability to fund religious education is not at issue and the primary concern is the regulatory system for determining the amount of funding and distributing it. These regulatory systems are beyond the scope of this book. In other systems, government funding for religious entities is prohibited by the constitution or other laws. In still other systems, funding is a highly complex legal question, the result of which can vary based on specific factors.

The first sort of system is reflected in many European countries. For example, in France private religious schools can receive government funding so long as they follow the same curriculum as public schools and submit to periodic inspections. This is so despite France's constitutional rule of *laïcité*. This funding is explicitly viewed as not violating the principle of *laïcité* because it does not favor religion or disfavor secularism, in that any religious school receiving public funding must teach the complete secular curriculum required of other schools. A school's religious

GOVERNMENT SUPPORT FOR RELIGION: FUNDING AND TAX   107

mission and religious education (or experience) cannot be used to reject or exclude the secular curriculum.

In Germany the government can fund churches and religious schools. Church funding has been highly controversial in recent years, but it has existed, and has been legal, for a long time. Religious schools can also receive state funding, but to do so in most circumstances they must be nonprofit and charge tuition at a level that does not exclude students based on economic class. This is because Germany has a guarantee of affordable education. Funding for churches and religious schools does not violate the German Constitution. There have, however, been attempts to pass laws that would prohibit funding for churches.

In many other countries in Europe, South America, and elsewhere, religious schools—and sometimes churches, synagogues, mosques, temples, and so on—can receive government funding. In many systems this is not particularly controversial, but requirements related to matters such as accessibility and curricular issues do exist in some of these systems.

The second sort of system is reflected in Japanese law. Under Article 20, and especially Article 89, of the Japanese Constitution, funding for religious entities is strongly prohibited. Yet Japanese funding for private education—including religious private education—falls somewhere between the European models discussed above and that of the US. All Japanese private schools recognized by the Ministry of Education, Culture, Sports, Science and Technology (MEXT) are able to receive some government support and religious schools are not automatically excluded from this support. Yet, unlike in many countries in Europe and in the US, in Japan religious schools make up only a small proportion of private schools. Regarding overall government funding for religion, the Japanese system is stricter than the current system in the US because over the past 20 years the United States Supreme Court has expanded access to funding for religious entities while Japan has continued to deny most such funding under its constitution. As a practical matter, the Japanese system strikes a better and more realistic balance between funding that is "generally available" and funding that specifically supports religious entities and religion than either the US or some European models.

In the US, until recently, government funding was primarily addressed under the Establishment Clause, but between 2017 and 2022 the United

108 ADVANCED INTRODUCTION TO LAW AND RELIGION

States Supreme Court decided three cases that dramatically changed that landscape and made the Free Exercise Clause a major focus in most funding cases. The cases are based on the Court's new interpretation of discrimination that violates the Free Exercise Clause.

Until 2002, certain things were clear under the Establishment Clause. Funding that could be used to pay for religious education, such as tuition vouchers or religious schoolteachers' pay programs, violated the Establishment Clause. In 2002, however, the Court decided *Zelman v Simmons-Harris*,[1] over a strong dissent. The *Zelman* court ruled in favor of a voucher program in Cleveland, Ohio which overwhelmingly benefited religious schools. The court held that the program did not violate the US Constitution's Establishment Clause because the parents chose to send their children to the religious schools and thus acted as a circuit breaker for the state action. In other words, since the state funds were allocated to religious schools to which the parents chose to send their kids, the money was allocated based on private choice rather than government choice. It did not matter that the money was paid directly to the schools so long as the parents chose to send their kids to those schools. As the dissent pointed out, for most parents the only practical choices for voucher funds were religious schools representing one or two Christian denominations, and in fact 96.4 per cent of voucher students attended these schools.

The *Zelman* decision broke with a long line of previous cases which had held that government could not use taxpayer dollars to fund religious education qua religious education. The Supreme Court's decision in *Zelman* upheld vouchers for religious schools, including those which proselytize; but *Zelman* did not say states *have to* fund these programs, only that they *can* fund them. This is where the Court's recent expansion of the Free Exercise Clause's antidiscrimination principle comes to the fore.

As was discussed in Chapter 2, the original case that defined the parameters of unconstitutional discrimination under the Free Exercise Clause was *Church of Lukumi Babalu Aye v City of Hialeah*, decided in 1993.[2] In that case the Court found the actions of the City of Hialeah, which involved overt discrimination and religious gerrymandering, were neither

---

[1]   536 U.S. 639 (2002).
[2]   508 U.S. 520, 533 (1993).

GOVERNMENT SUPPORT FOR RELIGION: FUNDING AND TAX 109

generally applicable nor neutral and therefore discriminated against the Santeria Church that brought the claim. The city passed an ordinance targeting the Santeria practice of animal sacrifice. The ordinance, while neutral on its face, only applied to Santeria practices and thus failed the neutrality requirement. The city did not allege an adequate compelling interest, and the ordinance was far from the least restrictive means of meeting the compelling interests alleged by the city.

For almost 25 years there were no US Supreme Court cases applying, and certainly none expanding, the *Lukumi Babalu Aye* approach. There were, however, several interesting lower court decisions. Then, in 2017, the Court decided *Trinity Lutheran v Comer*.[3] *Trinity Lutheran* and its progeny are also discussed in Chapter 2. In this chapter, however, the focus is on the cases' impact on Establishment Clause concerns over government funding.

In *Trinity Lutheran* the Court applied the neutrality concept to a situation where the law was not designed to harm the practice of religion, but rather denied religious entities access to a state benefit—playground chips recycled from tires under a state program—due to a clause in the state constitution. The Court held that this sort of denial, which was based on religious status, discriminates in violation of the neutrality principle and is therefore unconstitutional. In *Trinity Lutheran*, the neutrality principle went from protecting against religious discrimination that targets religious practices to creating a broad-based ban on differential treatment of religion even when the differential treatment is based on state establishment of religion concerns.

The holding in *Trinity Lutheran* stands for the notion that once the government opens a "public benefit" it cannot deny that benefit to a religious entity solely based on that entity's religious status. Moreover, a state cannot rely on its own state constitution to deny religious entities access to a public benefit because, according to the Court, any such denial violates the Free Exercise Clause of the US Constitution. If all "public benefits" that might qualify for this protection were as innocuous as playground resurfacing, *Trinity Lutheran* would seem an imminently reasonable decision. After all, denying access to funding for a primarily secular benefit simply because of the religious status of the entity seeking

---

[3]   582 U.S. ___ (2017).

110 ADVANCED INTRODUCTION TO LAW AND RELIGION

the benefit would smack of discrimination against religious entities and would seem an obvious violation of the Free Exercise Clause. Yet, where is the line to be drawn between public benefits that qualify for such protection and those that do not?

In *Espinoza v Montana Department of Revenue*, decided in 2020, the Court further expanded what counts as discrimination against religion under the Free Exercise Clause and made it harder for states to deny benefits to faith-based institutions, in a context far more troublesome than *Trinity Lutheran*. *Espinoza* involved a Montana tax credit program. The program provided a state tax credit to individuals or businesses that donated to recognized organizations providing scholarships for private schools. In turn, families could use the funds from the organizations for private school tuition and costs. Montana has a state constitutional amendment, reenacted in 1972, that prohibits state funds from supporting religious education. The Montana Department of Revenue created a rule that prohibited the tax credit from going to religious schools. The Montana Supreme Court held that the tax credit program violated the state constitution's no-aid-to-religious-schools provision. Importantly, however, rather than strike down the law only as applied to religious schools, the Montana Supreme Court held that the entire tax credit program was invalid. Therefore, since the program was invalidated in its entirety, no tax credit was available, regardless of the type of private school at which it would be used.

The US Supreme Court, over strong dissents, overturned the Montana Supreme Court decision and expanded the *Trinity Lutheran* decision. The Court held that the Montana no-aid provision as applied by the Montana Department of Revenue and the Montana Supreme Court discriminated based on religious status, in violation of the Free Exercise Clause. This decision was a dramatic expansion of the *Trinity Lutheran* reasoning because the tax credits supported scholarships that could be used to go to religious schools where the substance of the education is religious. That is, rather than funding playground chips that are not themselves religious, the tax credits could fund direct religious education in violation of the state's interest in remaining out of the religious funding game due to the divisiveness that it could create and due to the state's interest in public education.

The *Espinoza* ruling did leave the door ajar a little when it comes to limiting things such as tuition vouchers to religious private schools. The court drew a tightrope-like line between discrimination based on religious status—the fact that a school is religious—and situations where the denial of funding is based on concern that the funds will support religious functions. Any opening in this regard was slammed shut in *Carson v Makin*.[4]

Carson, decided in 2022, answered the question of whether states must include religious schools in tuition voucher programs. The case involved a program in Maine which paid for tuition at private schools where no public schools are available. Maine has vast areas with small populations and supporting public schools in those areas would be far more financially challenging than paying for students to attend private schools in these areas. Religious schools could participate in the program so long as they did not require students to take religion classes or participate in religious events. Thus, there was no status-based discrimination. The Court abandoned the status use distinction it created in *Trinity Lutheran* and expanded in *Espinoza* and essentially held that excluding religious entities from a public funding program based on status or use violates the antidiscrimination principle under the Free Exercise Clause. Thus, in the US today, funding religious entities is not only possible so long as the funding includes "private choice" but mandatory if the government creates any generally available funding program, and state concerns about establishment of religion do not matter because the US Constitution's Free Exercise Clause prevails over state concerns.

5.2   Tax exemptions and related benefits

Questions about tax exemptions for religious entities, religious property, and clergy have arisen at some point in nearly every system in the world. While this section will focus on the US system, which reflects a variety of approaches around the world, it will also look at the system in Singapore, which has some interesting provisions that are reflected in a variety of other systems and has also had several high-profile tax fraud prosecutions of religious entities. The primary focus of this section will be on taxation of religious non-profits; the section will also explore taxation of religious

---

[4]   ___ U.S. ___ (2022).

112 ADVANCED INTRODUCTION TO LAW AND RELIGION

property and clergy property owned by the religious entity (often referred to as a "parsonage").

In addition to the systems discussed in this section there are, of course, systems that do not tax favored religious entities, but might tax other religious entities. These systems are beyond the scope of this advanced introduction, but, interestingly, they are not limited to theocracies, as one might intuit. These systems can be found in a number of European countries, especially in Eastern Europe.

The US system is layered between federal, state, and local taxes. This section will focus on the federal taxation system except where explicitly stated otherwise. A number of complex issues arise when the Federal Internal Revenue Code (IRS Code) is applied to religious entities. The most common issues that arise involve religious entities and §501(c)(3) status. A number of issues have also arisen around the Federal Parsonage Exemption, and some commentators and tax lawyers have questioned the Parsonage Exemption's constitutionality.

Internal Revenue Code §501(c)(3) enables certain organizations to be federally tax-exempt. Moreover, donations to these organizations are deductible for the donor. Both of these are significant benefits to the qualifying organization, but to qualify for §501(c)(3), organizations must meet a number of criteria. A §501(c)(3) organization has to be "organized and operated exclusively" for an exempt purpose. Exempt purposes include religious, charitable, and educational purposes. Additionally, none of an exempt organization's net earnings can inure to the "benefit of any private shareholder or individual." This is commonly referred to as the "private inurement" requirement, and it has led to several issues in the context of religious organizations.

Another important requirement for §501(c)(3) status is that exempt organizations may not carry out political activity. This means that exempt organizations should not financially support or devote a substantial part of their activities to "carrying on propaganda, or otherwise attempting [...] to influence legislation." They may not "participate in or intervene in (including the publishing or distributing of statements) [...] any political campaign on behalf of (or in opposition to) any candidate for public office."

GOVERNMENT SUPPORT FOR RELIGION: FUNDING AND TAX   113

Cases involving religious organizations have arisen under each requirement. Therefore, there are cases addressing: (1) whether a religious organization is organized exclusively for an exempt purpose; (2) whether a religious organization is operated exclusively for an exempt purpose; (3) the meaning of, and relationship between, the terms "organized" and "operated"; (4) the meaning of "exclusively"; and of course what qualifies as an "exempt purpose" organization. Moreover, there are numerous cases on both the private inurement prohibition and the political activity prohibition. Each of these will be addressed in turn.

As mentioned above, a §501(c)(3) organization has to be "organized and operated exclusively" for an exempt purpose. Every element of this requirement is significant. Thus, the IRS and courts reviewing cases under this rule examine the meaning of "organized," "operated," "exclusively," and "exempt purpose." Every element must be met for an organization to qualify as a §501(c)(3) organization. Moreover, the inquiry into each element can be highly fact-sensitive.

Perhaps the most straightforward element is the last one, "exempt purpose." Generally, if an organization meets the other elements and it serves one of the purpose listed in §501(c)(3), it serves an exempt purpose. If it is not organized and operated for that purpose, however, it is not exempt under §501(c)(3).

To be "organized" for an exempt purpose the organization must demonstrate through documentation, such as articles of incorporation, trust instruments, charter, or bylaws, that it is organized to further charitable objectives meeting one or more of the exempt purposes specified in §501(c)(3). To be "operated" for an exempt purpose an organization must show that it in fact substantially operates for the purpose(s) for which it was organized. It must also show that it operates in the manner in which it was organized to operate. This has ramifications for the private inurement issues discussed later in this section. To be organized and operated "exclusively" for an exempt purpose, an organization seeking §501(c)(3) status must show it operates exclusively to fulfill an exempt purpose. This requires that its primary goal(s) is to carry out exempt activities. As a practical matter, however, "exclusively" in this context is not as strict as the common understanding of the term would suggest. Courts have interpreted this term loosely and have allowed entities to maintain or gain §501(c)(3) status even if they engage in some incidental activities that are

114 ADVANCED INTRODUCTION TO LAW AND RELIGION

not exempt, but these non-exempt activities cannot be a substantial or a primary focus of an exempt entity. If the non-exempt activity crosses the line so as to become substantial or primary, the entity will lose exempt status.

The requirement that none of an exempt organization's net earnings can inure to the "benefit of any private shareholder or individual" has led to a significant amount of litigation. Some cases are rather straightforward: for example, cases where those in charge of an organization, or members of their family, are paid far more than the fair market value of their services. Other cases are significantly harder: for example, a case where a church that has a sincerely held belief and tradition of caring for its members' spiritual and basic social needs provides health insurance for members at no cost to them. In the first line of cases the entity rarely is able to gain or maintain exempt status, but in the second situation the entity was allowed to keep its exempt status under §501(c)(3). Many cases, however, fall somewhere in between these two scenarios. Private inurement, like every other element under §501(c)(3), is a highly fact-sensitive issue.

Allowing private inurement, especially in the most egregious cases, would be inconsistent with the notion that §501(c)(3) entities serve the public good. Tax-exempt status in many systems is based on the notion that the entity receiving the exemption serves the public good, and this is true in the US system as well. Even if an entity serves the public good in some ways, if it allows private inurement it is questionable whether it is truly organized and run for exempt purposes. If a benefit is limited only to members of an organization private inurement is generally found because the class being served is not the "public." The amount of private inurement does not matter. Any private inurement violates the requirement.

In addition to the above-mentioned cases where compensation exceeding the fair market value of services provided was paid to interested individuals, cases in which private inurement has been found involve the provision of housing, personal expenses, food, cars, subsidized gifts, vacations, tuition payments, interest-free loans or grants, asset purchases, and several other benefits such as country club membership. Moreover, co-mingling of organizational funds and personal funds has been found to support a finding of private inurement.

There are cases, however, where courts or the IRS have found some private inurement to be acceptable because the private inurement is incidental to the organizations effectuating an exempt purpose. Thus, limiting burial at a religious cemetery only to co-religionists, the provision of medical benefits to church members pursuant to church doctrine requiring taking care of members' basic needs, and engaging in genealogical research for a specific religious group have not been deemed private inurement, even though only members benefit. This is because in each of these cases the courts and/or the IRS found that the private inurement was incidental to the exempt charitable/religious purpose of the entity. Thus, even though only co-religionists of the exempt organization benefited, the reason for that limitation was consistent with the exempt purpose of those organizations.

As one might expect given the private inurement requirement, an organization exempt under §501(c)(3) must maintain adequate financial records to demonstrate it meets all §501(c)(3) requirements. Moreover, a §501(c)(3) organization must file appropriate forms every year. "Churches" as defined by the IRS, however, are exempt from the annual reporting requirement. Because "churches"—as defined by the IRS—need not submit the same documentation as other 501(c)(3) entities, a number of interesting problems have arisen. This will be discussed a bit more below.

One of the most controversial requirements for religious organizations under §501(c)(3) is the requirement that §501(c)(3) organizations refrain from political activity and lobbying. There are three main areas of concern regarding this issue. The first is the specific §501(c)(3), and related regulatory, requirements regarding lobbying and political activity. This includes what is allowed, what is not allowed, and what remains unclear. It also includes what the IRS may do if a religious §501(c)(3) entity has been found in violation of the non-politicking requirement.

Second is whether such a requirement can be constitutional when a religious organization cannot separate its religious and political doctrines. The US Supreme Court has held that requiring §501(c)(3) religious entities to refrain from politics and lobbying is constitutional because of the §501(c)(4) alternative, but the Court has never addressed a situation where a religious entity's core religious values include issues such as pacifism or protecting the environment, and clergy give sermons around

116 ADVANCED INTRODUCTION TO LAW AND RELIGION

election time where these issues are addressed and one candidate clearly is on the opposite side.

Third is the relevance of §501(c)(4) to the question involved here. §501(c)(4) provides a mechanism by which a religious entity can engage in political activity and/or lobbying under certain carefully drawn circumstances without losing tax-exempt status. Yet, utilizing §501(c)(4) status has serious implications, because while the entity remains tax-exempt, donations to a §501(c)(4) entity are not tax-exempt.

§501(c)(3) organizations receive significant financial benefits both because the organization itself is tax-exempt and because donations to the organization are deductible for those making the donations. Suggested reasons for these benefits are that §501(c)(3) charitable organizations are non-profit and provide substantial benefits to society. The private inurement requirement discussed above helps assure a §501(c)(3) organization is non-profit and serves a public purpose. Refraining from political activity may also be consistent with serving society generally, but perhaps more importantly, since these organizations are tax-exempt and donations to them are deductible, the government has an interest in not subsidizing political activities through tax benefits given to charitable entities. Regardless of the reasons for the requirement that §501(c)(3) organizations refrain from political activity, the basic requirements have commanded a lot of attention in the regulations, cases, and commentary. In recent years there has been an organized effort by social conservatives to remove the requirement.

There are two types of requirements preventing a §501(c)(3) organization from engaging in politics. First, a §501(c)(3) organization may not engage in lobbying or attempting to influence legislation. Second, a §501(c)(3) organization may not participate or intervene in any political campaign. The latter requirement includes advocating for any candidate in a federal, state, or local election, and both requirements apply to federal, state, and local activity. This does not preclude issue advocacy so long as no candidate or party is supported. Thus, a religious organization exempt under §501(c)(3) that opposes or supports a woman's right to choose an abortion may address the issue of abortion from a religious perspective but may not lobby for legislation that supports its position or support a political candidate that agrees with its position.

GOVERNMENT SUPPORT FOR RELIGION: FUNDING AND TAX 117

§501(c)(3) addresses activities involving political campaigns in the following language: "[A §501(c)(3) organization may] not participate in or intervene in (including the publishing or distributing of statements), any political campaign on behalf of (or in opposition to) any candidate for public office." The Department of the Treasury regulations enforcing this provision make it clear that public office applies to any federal, state, or local office. Moreover, a candidate is anyone running for office, whether in a primary or general election, and whether self-declared or nominated by a political party. The regulations also make clear that participation in, or intervention in, a campaign through "publishing or distributing statements" includes both written and oral statements.

Thus, giving a sermon that advocates for a particular candidate or against a particular candidate, doing the same regarding a political party, inviting a specific candidate for election-related reasons, disseminating literature advocating for or against candidates, approving or disapproving of candidates in writing or verbally, and rating candidates—even in a nonpartisan manner—all violate the campaign requirement. It is important to note in regard to personal activities of organization leadership that a distinction is drawn between the personal activities of a §501(c)(3) organization's leaders and any activity that may be seen as coming from the organization. A sermon advocating for or against a candidate, distribution of political literature, or any other activity carrying the imprimatur of the §501(c)(3) entity violates the rule. Conversely, a clergy member or board member volunteering to help a campaign as an individual, while not holding themselves out as being affiliated with the §501(c)(3) entity, would not violate the rule, barring other circumstances that implicate the rule.

One of the toughest questions that arises is where the line lies between issue advocacy that does not involve lobbying and that which impacts campaigns, when a particular candidate or candidates clearly fall on the wrong or the right side of these issues. The IRS has noted that in the context of political campaigns, as in lobbying, it "depends upon all of the facts and circumstances of each case."

Another tough issue is candidate appearances at the §501(c)(3) organization or organization sponsored events. This is also addressed in IRS Revenue Ruling 2007-41. Inviting a political candidate to speak is not a per se violation of the campaign rule, but it carries significant risks if the IRS finds it to be partisan or otherwise taking any position on an election.

118 ADVANCED INTRODUCTION TO LAW AND RELIGION

The IRS will look at several factors in analyzing whether a candidate appearance violates the campaign rule. There are three main factors listed that the IRS considers, but the ruling makes clear that the list is not exhaustive. First, did the organization give equal opportunities for opposing candidates for the same position to participate at the appearance? Second, did the organization indicate its opposition or support for the candidate that appeared there? Third, was political fundraising conducted at the event where the candidate appeared?

A related issue arises if the organization invites a candidate to speak, but not in their capacity as a candidate. The key question here is whether the candidate is "publicly recognized" by the organization as a candidate in relation to the appearance (including before and after the appearance). If a candidate, for example, is an author and is invited to speak about a book they wrote, and no mention is made of their candidacy, there would not likely be a problem under §501(c)(3). In contrast, if the person was invited as an author and candidate for X office a violation is far more likely to be found. Significantly, there are some election-related activities that do not violate §501(c)(3). For example, educating people on their right to vote, "get out the vote" efforts, and voter registration initiatives are allowed so long as they are not done in a manner that advocates for or against a specific candidate, issue, or party.

If a religious entity wants to maintain tax-exempt status while engaging in politics. §501(c)(4) is an option. In *Regan v Taxation with Representation*,[5] the United States Supreme Court upheld the lobbying restrictions under §501(c)(3) in part because §501(c)(4) provides a valid alternative for entities which promote social welfare and want to engage in some forms of political activity while maintaining tax-exempt status. There are, however, some significant differences between §501(c)(3) and (4) entities. First, §501(c)(4) entities are themselves exempt from taxation, but donations to those entities are not deductible for donors. Second, §501(c)(4) entities, for purposes relevant to the current discussion of religious entities, must be "operated exclusively for the promotion of social welfare."

In general, an organization is operated exclusively for the promotion of social welfare if it is primarily engaged in promoting in some way the common good and general welfare of the people of the community.

---

[5]   461 U.S. 540 (1983).

GOVERNMENT SUPPORT FOR RELIGION: FUNDING AND TAX 119

An organization embraced within this section is one which is operated primarily for the purpose of bringing about civic betterments and social improvements. Many religious entities can meet the social welfare requirement. First, many religious entities offer services to the community, such as food banks, shelters, and the like, that would easily qualify as promoting social welfare. Second, it could be argued that religious entities serve the social welfare of the community simply by functioning as religious entities.

Another issue that has arisen regarding religious organizations under the IRS Code and regulations is the questions of "church status." "Churches," which includes all houses of worship regardless of religion, are treated differently from other organizations, including other religious organizations, under §501(c)(3). The term "church status" is awkward because it applies not just to churches, but to synagogues, temples, mosques, and so on. The most significant differences between "churches" and other religious charities are that churches are not required to receive a ruling from the IRS to gain §501(c)(3) status, churches need not file annual informational returns or forms to maintain §501(c)(3) status, churches need not file reports other §501(c)(3) entities are required to file, and there are significant restrictions on the IRS's ability to investigate churches and specific procedures the IRS must follow if it does investigate a church. Of course, if the IRS chooses to investigate and finds that an entity claiming church status does not meet the requirements to hold that status, the IRS may revoke church status. If an entity loses church status it may still remain a §501(c)(3) entity so long as it meets all the requirements to qualify and maintain such status, including the filing of annual reports.

Two major questions arise in regard to church status. First, what are the requirements to maintain church status? This question may seem odd since churches can simply declare themselves so and do not need IRS approval to be considered a church for §501(c)(3) purposes, but of course, the IRS may challenge that status, and then the question becomes highly relevant. This question also raises significant constitutional concerns. Second, what procedures are churches entitled to if the IRS chooses to challenge church status? This second question is beyond the scope of this book.

Church status is mentioned in 26 U.S.C. §170(b)(1)(A)(I), which is part of a broader provision addressing deductions for individual contributions

120 ADVANCED INTRODUCTION TO LAW AND RELIGION

to charitable entities. Yet, the term "church" is not defined in that section. Religious entities need not apply for church status, but when that status is questioned by the IRS, two approaches have generally been used to analyze whether an entity should be able to maintain church status. The first is a set of 14 criteria set forth by the IRS. The second is referred to as the Associational Test. The two approaches overlap in significant ways.

The 14 criteria are: (1) a distinct legal existence; (2) a recognized creed and form of worship; (3) a definite and distinct ecclesiastical government; (4) a formal code of doctrine and discipline; (5) a distinct religious history; (6) a membership not associated with any other church or denomination; (7) an organization of ordained ministers; (8) ordained ministers selected after completing prescribed studies; (9) a literature of its own; (10) established places of worship; (11) regular congregations; (12) regular religious services; (13) Sunday schools for religious instruction of the young; and (14) schools for the preparation of its ministers.

The Associational Test requires that a church be a group of believers who regularly meet for "communal worship." Thus, courts using the "associational" approach look at whether individuals associate with each other for worship. Many courts refer to both the 14 criteria and the Associational Test, but in recent years the Associational Test has become more dominant in judicial opinions. The IRS still considers both the 14 criteria and the associational aspects of an entity. As several courts have pointed out it is fair to say that the two approaches would often lead to the same results because the most salient of the 14 criteria relate to the associational nature of a church.

It is hard to ignore the fact that both these approaches point toward what many would consider "traditional" churches and congregations. In fact, courts have held that churches that use broadcast media, mailings, the internet, and other nontraditional means of assembly are not entitled to "church" status under the IRC. Courts have also required that churches "regularly" meet for worship, so occasionally meeting for worship has been held not to qualify, especially when a number of the other indicia mentioned in the 14 criteria are missing.

Given the benefits bestowed by "church" status, one would think the act of defining what is and what is not a church by the IRS and courts would violate the Establishment Clause and/or Free Exercise Clause. Yet, courts have repeatedly held that because church status simply allows entities not to have to file formally to be given §501(c)(3) status and not to have to file annual forms, it helps prevent government involvement with religious entities. Moreover, courts have held that since religious entities that are not "churches" can still maintain §501(c)(3) status, the exception to the filing requirements for "churches" is not the sort of benefit that gives rise to violations under the Free Exercise or Establishment Clauses.

As a number of commentators and judges have pointed out, however, this is quite disturbing because it puts courts and the IRS in the business of deciding what a "church" is, even if only for limited purposes. This is especially problematic when one considers that only "churches" are excluded from the filing requirements.. All other §501(c)(3) entities, whether religious or not, must file the paperwork. Thus, the argument favoring exemptions for religious entities under §501(c)(3) in the face of Establishment Clause concerns—that religious entities are only one of many types of non-profit entities that serve a variety of communities— does not apply to the "church" status benefits.

Another issue that has arisen under federal law is the "Parsonage Exemption." It is important to note that many states and localities also have parsonage exemptions, and the vast array of these exemptions are beyond the scope of this book. The Federal Parsonage Exemption is a provision—or really two provisions—under the Internal Revenue Code that exempts property from gross income for ministers of the gospel for purposes of calculating income tax. These provisions are found in IRC §107. The first provision exempts the value of a home provided by the church to ministers. The second provision exempts from income "the rental allowance paid" to a minister "to the extent such allowance does not exceed the fair rental value of the home, including furnishings and appurtenances such as a garage, plus the cost of utilities."

The term "minister of the gospel" is obviously under-inclusive, since the use of the terms 'minister' and "gospel" are from Protestant conceptions of clergy (that is, the term minister of the gospel is used rather than the terms priest, rabbi, imam, and so on). The term has been interpreted by courts and in Treasury regulations, however, to apply to all clergy who are serving in a ministerial role. An IRS Revenue Ruling states that functions performed by a "minister of the gospel" are "the performance of sacerdotal functions, the conduct of religious worship, the administration

122 ADVANCED INTRODUCTION TO LAW AND RELIGION

and maintenance of religious organizations and their integral agencies, and the performance of teaching and administrative duties at theological seminaries." The IRS and courts have excluded even ordained clergy who do not meet these requirements.

Regulations enacted by the Department of Treasury explain what the term "home" means. The regulations state that the home includes not only the "dwelling place" but also all furnishings within the home and attachments, such as garages. This is applied to both provisions in IRC §107, but also reflects the language from subsection 2 which applies the housing allowance to "the fair rental value of the home, including furnishings and appurtenances such as a garage, plus the cost of utilities." Moreover, the cost of utilities may be covered.

The regulations make clear, however, that any housing or housing allowance provided by the religious entity to a minister must be compensation for their services and not simply an extra perk. The religious entity has a number of ways to formally declare the housing or housing allowance is compensation for service being rendered by the minister. The most obvious way to do this is in the minister's employment contract, but it may also be done through other official documents, such as minutes or resolutions by the religious entity.

The Parsonage Exemption, and especially the regulations used to interpret and enforce it, raise serious constitutional questions under the Establishment Clause. There is no clear answer from the US Supreme Court or Federal Appellate Courts to these questions yet, but in a carefully reasoned decision in the United States District Court for the Western District of Wisconsin, the court held the Parsonage Exemption violates the Establishment Clause.[6] For those interested in these issues it is worth looking at the above referenced decision and at the law review articles that address the constitutionality of the Parsonage Exemption.

While the US system is among the most complex due to the intricacies of §501(c)(3), it is not the only system that has provided tax benefits to

---

[6]   *Freedom from Religion Found., Inc. v. Lew*, 983 F. Supp. 2d 1051, 1054 (W.D. Wis., 2013). This decision was vacated in 2014 on standing grounds by the United States Court of Appeals for the Seventh Circuit, but that court did not address the constitutionality of the parsonage exemption.

GOVERNMENT SUPPORT FOR RELIGION: FUNDING AND TAX 123

religious entities as charitable institutions. Singapore has a system reflective of numerous other countries' systems and has undertaken several high-profile tax fraud prosecutions of religious entities. The Singaporean system for religious tax exemptions is fascinating, as are the high-profile prosecutions of those who violate the rules prohibiting personal gain. Perhaps the most notable of these prosecutions is the *City Harvest Church* case.[7]

Under Singaporean law, religious organizations are subject to the Societies Act, under which they register with a government agency known as the Registrar of Societies and are required to file an annual financial report with the government. The Societies Act does not provide all societies with tax exemptions. To gain a tax exemption, a charity—including religious organizations—must apply for and be granted "charity status." The "advancement of religion" is a charitable purpose similar to §501(c)(3) in the US. If an organization is granted charitable status, it is exempt not only from income taxes, but also from property taxes. Any society that gains this tax exemption must file an audited report annually. These reports have to be carefully prepared and meet strict rules. This is, of course, quite different from (and one might say better than) the lack of reporting for entities that receive "church status" under §501(c)(3) in the US.

Charities may invest some funds—but not a significant amount—in non-charitable activities, but anything earned is not considered part of the charitable purpose and is therefore taxable. Moreover, any such investment must be made under a separate entity from the charity itself. This is similar to §501(c)(3). Singapore's system, while having some similarities to that of the US, has several important requirements not found in the US system. Also, prosecutors in Singapore have been more willing to prosecute charities that abuse the tax exemption system than are prosecutors in many other countries. Even so, a violation has to be pretty significant to warrant prosecution in Singapore.

---

[7] *Public Prosecutor v Lam Leng Hung and others* [2015] SGDC 326. This case has a substantial appellate history on the length of the criminal sentences.

6. Religious autonomy

6.1 Introduction

The doctrine of religious autonomy is one of the central elements of law and religion. It involves a wide range of issues addressing the autonomy of religious bodies and individuals from government interference. Questions such as whether civil courts can decide religious disputes; whether civil employment laws can impact the hiring, retention, or firing of clergy; who has liability for torts such as sexual or physical abuse by clergy—all fall under the concept of religious autonomy. Different systems have come to different conclusions on these issues, but the issues go to the core of the freedom of religious entities and individuals to follow the tenets of their faith without government interference, as well as whether civil authority can have any role in governing religious entities' conduct given important legal rules and social norms in the relevant nation. This chapter will address the role of civil authorities in addressing religious property disputes and schisms; the hiring, firing, and supervision of clergy; and questions surrounding the role of civil authorities in dealing with issues such as clergy abuse.

6.2 Intrareligious disputes

Intrareligious disputes are often referred to as "schisms." These disputes often involve battles over real property and sometimes funds or chattel property, but not all religious schisms involve property disputes. In many systems the key question in intrareligious disputes is whether government can get involved in resolving the dispute, and if so, to what extent. The number of approaches to this question around the world are staggering.

They range from systems in which the government can directly resolve the dispute to systems where the government—including courts—must refrain from answering ecclesiastical questions. The latter systems raise a wide range of issues, such as: What counts as an ecclesiastical question? Must the government refrain totally from resolving these disputes? If not, what are the limits on government decision making? If so, is there any neutral body that can resolve these disputes?

There have been thousands of cases addressing these issues in the US, so we will begin with the US system and the ecclesiastical abstention doctrine. This will be followed by discussion of other systems, at which point the primary focus will be on Japan because it has a well-structured Religious Juridical Persons Act that reflects the approaches of many systems around the world.

In the US, intrareligious disputes are directly impacted by the role and jurisdiction of federal and state courts. The central principle in the US context is that state and federal courts do not involve themselves in ecclesiastical disputes. Courts may, however, address issues concerning civil or property rights, as long as they need not resolve ecclesiastical issues in order to do so. This rule raises numerous questions, and several settled principles of law have arisen as a result, but different jurisdictions have sometimes interpreted these rules in different ways. For the most part, each question that arises seems to garner a majority approach and several minority approaches that are generally closely related to the majority approach.

An important note is that intrareligious disputes in the US are often referred to as "church property disputes" and "church schisms." This terminology was adopted in the nineteenth century and has stuck. The terminology is vastly underinclusive because the same rules that apply to churches apply to synagogues, mosques, temples, and other houses of worship or loci of religious entities. I reluctantly use the traditional US terminology when discussing US law because it makes it easier to discuss the US rule, but I note that the under-inclusiveness of the terminology is highly uncomfortable.

One of the first issues addressed by most US jurisdictions in church property and church schism cases is: What kind of religious institution is involved? Is it hierarchical or congregational? If the former, what is its

126 ADVANCED INTRODUCTION TO LAW AND RELIGION

structure? If the latter, how does it govern itself? The next question that is often asked is whether the issue involved in the case requires the determination of ecclesiastical matters. If so, the courts generally find they have no jurisdiction. If not, the analysis generally continues.

Church property disputes often involve church schisms, but property cases are frequently held to be addressable by the courts using either neutral principles of law or another acceptable method. Church schism cases that do not involve property can involve a variety of issues such as employment disputes, disputes over membership status, disputes over control of the church, and disputes over financial matters. Significantly, the law addressing church property disputes is frequently used in church schism cases, so this section will first address church property disputes and then move on to schisms.

The most recognized rule applicable to church property disputes comes from *Watson v Jones*,[1] decided by the US Supreme Court in 1871. The *Watson* case involved a dispute over church property at the Walnut Street Presbyterian Church, which was located in the state of Kentucky. The ultimate question was which of two factions claiming to have authority to control church property was entitled to exercise that authority. The dispute arose over the Civil War and the issue of slavery. The General Assembly of the Presbyterian Church denounced slavery and required those who aided the Confederacy or who supported slavery to repent, and both the Louisville Presbytery and the Synod of Kentucky split over this issue. In the case of the Walnut Street Church, those who wanted to leave the national church sought and obtained admission to a newly formed entity, the Presbyterian Church of the Confederacy. The schism in the Walnut Street Church arose as a result of these events.

The US Supreme Court ultimately had to determine which of these two factions was entitled to control the church property as the properly constituted Walnut Street Church, and as the Court explained in its decision, it had to do so without determining purely ecclesiastical matters; that is, the Court could address civil and property rights in a church dispute, but only to the extent that it did not have to determine ecclesiastical issues in the process. In an oft-quoted passage that has stood as a fundamental

---

[1]   80 U.S. 679 (1871).

tenet of the law applicable to church property disputes, the Court held the following:

> The questions which have come before civil courts concerning the rights to property held by ecclesiastical bodies, may [...] be profitably classified under three general heads.
> 1. The first of these is when the property which is the subject of the controversy has been, by the deed or will of the donor, or other instrument by which the property is held, by the express terms of the instrument devoted to the teaching, support, or spread of some specific form of religious doctrine or belief.
> 2. The second is when the property is held by a religious congregation which, by the nature of its organization, is strictly independent of other ecclesiastical associations, and so far as church government is concerned, owes no fealty or obligation to any higher authority.
> 3. The third is where the religious congregation or ecclesiastical body holding the property is but a subordinate member of some general church organization in which there are superior ecclesiastical tribunals with a general and ultimate power of control more or less complete, in some supreme judicatory over the whole membership of that general organization.[2]

The Court held that the Presbyterian Church was in the third category (that is, it is a hierarchical church) and held that in this category civil courts should defer to the decision of the highest church judicatory "to which the matter has been carried." Moreover, the Court held that the second category (that is, congregational churches) should be governed "by the ordinary principles that govern voluntary associations," which frequently are governed by majority rule or which vest control in congregational officers. It is important to note at this point that another important approach based on "neutral principles of law" has been added to the fray. In *Watson*, the Court deferred to the decision of the original church hierarchy, which vested control in the faction that did not seek to leave the church. The other faction, the Court held, had in effect abandoned its right to control church property by splitting off into a new church against the will of the original church's hierarchy.

Each of the three Watson categories has given rise to numerous cases in the US, so a brief overview of this law is helpful to anyone seeking an advanced introduction to this law.

---

[2]   *Id.* at 722–23.

128 ADVANCED INTRODUCTION TO LAW AND RELIGION

Category 1: Express and implied trusts

The first category of situations involved in church property disputes set forth by the *Watson* Court consists of express trusts and similar devises reflecting the express will of the donor to give the property for a specified use or to devote it to the propagation of a specific faith or set of doctrines. Many states' courts still require an express trust or similar legally valid document reflecting the will of the donor. A few jurisdictions also recognize implied trusts as valid evidence that church property was intended for a specific use or to support a particular faith or set of religious commitments. Several jurisdictions generally fit within the first group of jurisdictions but have recognized a limited number of circumstances where an implied trust will be recognized.

One of the most common questions that arises in trust cases is how to approach a situation where the donor sets forth an intent that a property should be used for the propagation of a specific sect and the document of conveyance mentions specific doctrines of that sect, but in subsequent years the sect changes some of the relevant doctrines. Most courts addressing this issue have held that the donor understood that the sect might alter some doctrines in the future and as long as the church is still a member of the specified sect, the grant of the property to that sect remains valid. Another variation on this theme is where the sect itself merges with another sect or sects. In such situations many courts look to whether the new entity reflects the faith specified in the trust, but they do so without determining ecclesiastical questions. That is, they must determine if the new entity is consistent with the old, but must often rely on the actions of the new entity in order to make these determinations. Some jurisdictions use the concept of implied trust to deal with changes to church doctrine or polity that may not have been foreseen by the conveyor of an express trust. A few eschew the distinction between implied and express trusts and focus solely on the intent of the conveyance as set forth in the language of relevant documents and in other relevant evidence of the intent of the donor.

Category 2: Congregational churches

The general rule for determining who governs and controls property in congregational churches is roughly that set forth in *Watson*. Most courts recognize the will of the majority of these congregations unless the congregation has created an alternative governance structure through a constitution, bylaws, or other governing document adopted by the congregation. Courts frequently apply neutral principles of law, as discussed later, to church property disputes. Importantly, one of the neutral principles many courts have applied is that of the governance structure and governing documents of the congregation, which is also important under the *Watson* approach to congregational churches. Therefore, in some cases the doctrine from *Watson* is implicitly woven together with the neutral principles of law concept, whereas in other cases this connection is explicit. Without addressing ecclesiastical matters, courts will look to the secular indicia of property ownership and control, such as deeds, church governance documents, state property law, and wills and trusts granting the property.

Most courts will go to great lengths to avoid hearing ecclesiastical questions because it has long been held that civil courts have no jurisdiction over such matters. As a practical matter, however, it is sometimes hard to determine where the secular ends and the ecclesiastical begins, so the majority of courts defer to congregational decisions and/or secular documents and will only get involved in questioning congregational decisions when the procedure used to reach such decisions is contrary to church governance documents or, in some cases, state law governing charitable and/or religious corporations. When the dispute is over who constitutes the congregation, courts generally will defer to the body or faction that constitutes the majority of a congregational church. This enables courts to answer the civil law questions without making religious determinations. A small minority of jurisdictions, however, focus on which parties continue to follow the religious principles held by the congregational church prior to the schism or other events giving rise to the property dispute. They do so without determining the validity or nature of such principles, but still in these jurisdictions the principles in place prior to the property dispute remain an important focus.

In such jurisdictions, the courts do not claim to have jurisdiction over ecclesiastical matters but rather argue that religious doctrine may be explored to validate civil and property rights. The courts do not analyze the doctrines for their religious significance but rather for what they say about the civil or property rights involved. Therefore, these courts leave the ecclesiastical doctrines as they found them, only using these doctrines as understood before the dispute began in order to determine civil or property rights. It should be obvious that these jurisdictions come much closer to the secular–ecclesiastical dispute line than most jurisdictions and therefore increase the risk of impacting religious decisions and/ or doctrines, albeit unintentionally. Every jurisdiction has rejected on Establishment and Free Exercise Clause grounds the old English rule that allowed civil courts to make ecclesiastical decisions. Given First Amendment concerns, jurisdictions in the United States are uniform in their rejection of the ability to decide ecclesiastical disputes.

Category 3: Hierarchical churches

Hierarchical churches are, as the term suggests, churches with formal hierarchies. The most obvious examples include the Roman Catholic Church, Eastern Orthodox Churches, the Episcopalian Church and the Presbyterian Church. There are a number of others. These churches share several traits that place them in this category. As will be seen, however, there are some churches that do not fit neatly into this category, but which have nonetheless been considered hierarchical by courts.

The factors most often used by courts to determine that a given church is hierarchical include whether there are ecclesiastical courts that can bind churches and church members; whether there is a general set of rules and procedures that purports to bind individual churches within the broader church; whether a church has bound itself in some way to a national, regional, or international body; whether religious precepts are dictated by some centralized body; and whether a centralized body has the authority to appoint or remove clergy. Some churches share all these traits and thus are easily categorized as hierarchical, whereas others may share only one or a few of these traits, thus requiring courts to make the decision whether a church is hierarchical for civil law purposes based on all the relevant facts.

If a church is hierarchical, courts generally defer to the decisions of the highest authority within the church hierarchy. This ostensibly prevents civil courts from having to make ecclesiastical determinations in such cases. As noted earlier, courts cannot determine ecclesiastical questions without running afoul of the Establishment and Free Exercise Clauses of the First Amendment to the United States Constitution. Some scholars have suggested that this deference may itself interfere with First Amendment rights, and some courts avoid using categories such as hierarchical or congregational, instead relying on neutral principles of law to determine church property disputes. Even then, some of the factors relevant to determining whether or not a given church is hierarchical can be used as neutral principles of law. Not surprisingly, a number of jurisdictions use both approaches in determining church property disputes. These jurisdictions frequently apply neutral principles to determine property disputes, but whether or not a church is congregational or hierarchical influences the principles applied and their application.

The key to analysis of property disputes within hierarchical churches is complete deference to the highest judicial authority within the general church. Courts still must determine whether a church is hierarchical in the first place and who the highest authority is, but usually these things are reasonably clear from the documents, traditions, and/or practices within the broader church. Where this is not clear, courts generally avoid determining any ecclesiastical questions and use secular criteria based on the evidence to decide who is the highest authority within a church. Courts use similar mechanisms when there are internal struggles within the church as to who represents the hierarchy, such as cases where two bishops claim to control a given locale. In such cases, courts will look to the history of the dispute, church governance documents, statements of high-ranking church officials as to who is the proper authority, and the overall governance system of the church. In doing so, courts avoid purely ecclesiastical questions and take the preceding evidence at face value. Courts do sometimes determine whether church hierarchies have followed their own procedural rules in determining property disputes, but these courts do not pass judgment on the substantive correctness of the hierarchies' decisions.

For nearly 100 years, courts generally followed the approach set forth in *Watson v Jones* in church property dispute cases. In 1969, however, in *Presbyterian Church in U.S. v Mary Elizabeth Blue Hull Memorial Presbyterian Church*,[3] the Supreme Court referred to "neutral principles of law" that could be applied to church property disputes. The language was basically dicta, but the Georgia Supreme Court—whose decision was at issue in that case—as well as some other state courts began to apply neutral principles to church property disputes. The next year, in *Maryland and Virginia Eldership of the Churches of God v Church of God*

---

[3]   393 U.S. 440 (1969).

132 ADVANCED INTRODUCTION TO LAW AND RELIGION

at Sharpsburg, Inc.,[4] the Court again approvingly referred to "neutral principles of law." In 1979, in *Jones v Wolf*,[5] a case from Georgia—a state that had begun applying neutral principles after the Court's decision in *Mary Elizabeth Hull*—the Court formally acknowledged that a neutral principles approach was both constitutional and beneficial in deciding church property disputes.

Neutral principles are a mechanism courts can use to avoid getting involved in ecclesiastical questions, including those related to the governance of churches. Thus, the Court held that neutral principles are consistent with the longstanding principle that civil courts cannot determine ecclesiastical issues without running afoul of the Free Exercise and Establishment Clauses, and in fact a neutral principles approach will better avoid approaching the boundary between secular and ecclesiastical matters than the traditional approach. Moreover, a neutral principles approach that relies on deeds, state corporation law, trust documents, church bylaws, and so on would allow hierarchical as well as congregational churches to spell out the ownership of church property before disputes arise, thus essentially predetermining the outcomes in these types of cases.

Since *Jones v Wolf* was decided, more and more courts have adopted a neutral principles approach, either by itself or in conjunction with the categories set forth in *Watson v Jones*. Today, most jurisdictions rely on a neutral principles of law approach to some degree or another. Still, some jurisdictions have rejected the neutral principles approach because it was not mandated by the Court. As noted earlier, a large number of jurisdictions have combined the traditional approach from *Watson v Jones* with the neutral principles of law approach. There is language from *Jones v Wolf* which directly supports deference to an "authoritative ecclesiastical body" in cases where church documents or other "instruments of ownership" incorporate religious concepts. The reason for this is that, as noted earlier, civil courts cannot determine ecclesiastical matters without running afoul of the First Amendment.

Some examples of the sorts of documents or rules that constitute neutral principles of law are deeds, trust documents, other documents of con-

---

4   393 U.S. 367 (1970).
5   443 U.S. 595 (1979).

RELIGIOUS AUTONOMY   133

veyance such as wills, church constitutions, church bylaws, and/or state corporation laws relevant to church incorporation (assuming that the church is incorporated). This list is not exhaustive given the many varying factual scenarios in such cases, but it does represent factors that have been considered in the vast majority of intrareligious dispute cases applying neutral principles of law. The idea, as noted earlier, is that civil courts can use these neutral principles to determine church property disputes in the same manner as most other property disputes, without delving into ecclesiastical concerns.[6]

The law governing church schisms is intertwined with that applicable to church property disputes. This makes sense because most church property disputes themselves arise as the result of a schism within a church. Thus, neutral principles and the hierarchical–congregational approach can be sensibly applied in the church schism context. Moreover, the constitutional duty civil courts have to avoid becoming involved in determining ecclesiastical issues is equally applicable—if not more so—in the church schism context. It should be obvious that church property disputes are often a type of church schism case, but given the significant attention paid to property disputes by civil courts, property disputes have essentially become a category in and of themselves. Non-property-oriented schism cases most often involve disputes between church factions over issues such as retention or termination of clergy or other church employees, dismissal of church members from membership, calls for financial accounting within the church, questions over who controls church governance, and cases where churches or factions within churches seek to affiliate with another denomination or where churches or factions within them seek to disaffiliate from a denomination.

---

[6]   There are also a small number of cases that rely exclusively on state incorporation laws without addressing neutral principles or any other constitutionally driven test. These cases are arguably de facto neutral principle cases even if they never raise the issue. Most cases looking at state incorporation laws do so in the context of neutral principles analysis, where the state laws are used to determine who controls church property and other assets. As with other neutral principles, the state laws serve as a mechanism for helping to determine church property disputes without delving into ecclesiastical questions. In the end, this is the primary goal of a neutral principles approach regardless of which specific principle or principles courts rely on.

134 ADVANCED INTRODUCTION TO LAW AND RELIGION

The central tenet of church schism cases is that civil courts will not get involved in deciding ecclesiastical matters, but courts can decide some intrareligious dispute questions as long as they can do so without deciding ecclesiastical questions. This rule has significant implications for cases involving disputes over clergy employment and cases involving church membership. Any substantive decisions on these matters are beyond the jurisdiction of civil courts. Courts may, however, look at the processes applied to clergy employment and membership expulsion issues to make sure that the church followed its own procedural rules.

Even if a court finds that a church failed to follow its own procedures, the court will simply undo the procedurally flawed decision and leave it to the church to follow its own procedures in potentially arriving at the same decision. Most courts avoid delving into church procedure when in order to do so the court would need to address ecclesiastical issues. Some courts will go further than others by more narrowly defining "ecclesiastical" in these cases.

Outside of the US, Japan provides an excellent example of a different approach to intrareligious disputes. The Japanese approach is also reflected in numerous other systems in Europe, Asia, and elsewhere. In Japan many, but not all, intrareligious disputes are covered under the Religious Juridical Persons Act (宗教法人法 *Shuukyou Houjin Hou*). Religions do not need to register under the Act, but if they do register most intrareligious disputes would be decided by the incorporation requirements under the Act. For example, Chapter III of the Act sets forth rules for representative officers and responsible officers. These officers are responsible for making decisions for the organization under the Act. They are not responsible for making religious decisions, but due to the way in which incorporation is carried out under the Act they would be able to decide things such as disposition of property in a property dispute.

Incorporation under the Act governs many issues and there are specific provisions on the dispossession or sale of both real and chattel property, merger with another religious entity, and dissolution of the religious entity, among other situations. Rules of incorporation under the Act can be changed but the procedures for doing so are set forth under the Act. The key is that the Act treats religious entities that incorporate under it as corporations, so that corporate structure, bylaws, rules, and so on help avoid or govern the outcome of most intrareligious disputes. Since the

Act does not govern ecclesiastical questions, the religions remain free to make any and all decisions about religious matters, but if disputes arise as to property, merger, dissolution, and so on, the Act governs those issues. There is no requirement, however, that religions register under the Act, and for those that do not—and even for those that do, if they choose to challenge a decision by the representative or responsible officers—these disputes may still end up in court. However, that it is relatively rare in Japan and courts endeavor to avoid ecclesiastical questions, relying on something akin to neutral principles when it is possible to do so. The Act, of course, provides many such principles if litigation ensues after a decision is made by a registered religious entity. A large number of other countries have similar systems, but Japan's Religious Juridical Persons Act is one of the most detailed laws, and also one of the laws least likely to interfere with ecclesiastical decisions.

6.3 Hiring, supervision, and retention of clergy and others

In the US, civil courts have repeatedly held that it is inappropriate to question church decisions regarding the employment of clergy, barring a procedural issue. The reason for this is quite simple: the hiring and firing of clergy is central to the religious aspects of a church because the role of clergy is central to the religious functioning of most religious institutions. It is therefore nearly impossible to separate out ecclesiastical concerns when deciding these cases.

A central aspect of this is a concept called the "ministerial exception." The ministerial exception means that civil government—including the courts—cannot interfere with a religious entity's decisions about the hiring, retention, or firing of clergy members because to do so would often require answering ecclesiastical questions or interfering with the religious decisions of an entity. Doing so would violate the Establishment Clause and the Free Exercise Clause of the First Amendment. Until 2012, however, it was widely thought that the ministerial exception applied only to clergy or those with clear religious authority.

136 ADVANCED INTRODUCTION TO LAW AND RELIGION

In 2012, however, in *Hosanna-Tabor Evangelical Lutheran Church v Equal Employment Opportunity Commission*,[7] the US Supreme Court held that a "called" teacher could be fired by a religious school because she occupied a role with important religious functions, and that the very nature of being "called" itself rendered her position religious. She had been fired under circumstances that would normally have raised valid claims for disability discrimination and retaliation under the Americans with Disabilities Act. The church and its religious school, however, had longstanding doctrines that disputes should be handled internally, and that outside litigation violates church tenets. They argued that the teacher was fired for violating these doctrines. The Court held that it could not question the church school's decision under these circumstances because the teacher was a minister for purposes of the ministerial exception, but also held that the situation might be different for a non-called teacher or other employee who was not a minister. There was also a debate between the Justices about whether the determination of who counts as a minister for purposes of the ministerial exception is a functional question or one of complete deference to the religious entity, because different religions view the concept of a "minister" broadly or narrowly.

In 2020, the US Supreme Court expanded the ministerial exception further in *Our Lady of Guadalupe School v Morrissey-Berru*.[8] In that case two teachers at two different religious schools filed claims that they were fired based on disability in violation of the Americans with Disabilities Act and because of age in violation of the Age Discrimination in Employment Act, respectively. Unlike the teacher in *Hosanna-Tabor*, these teachers had less clear religious duties and were primarily involved in teaching secular subjects. The Court held that the test for deciding who qualifies as a minister requires great deference to the religious entity, and while the functions of the employee are important in determining who is a minister, that calculus is not a formulaic test. The Court held that the primary function of many religious schools is the religious development and education of their students and that decisions about the hiring and retention of teachers go to the core of that religious mission. Therefore, the teachers could not prevail in their claims because the ministerial exception applies.

---

[7]   565 U.S. 171 (2012).

[8]   591 U.S. ___ (2020).

RELIGIOUS AUTONOMY 137

When, however, there are established church procedures regarding employment decisions or, in a few cases, where the clergy member has a contractual right to pay or certain procedural safeguards, courts sometimes will decide these issues without addressing the substantive merits of the employment decision. If a court needs to address the latter to determine the former, most jurisdictions refuse to hear the case.

In a few cases, the procedure for calling meetings is set forth in bylaws or articles of incorporation under state incorporation laws, and those laws become relevant to whether the church followed appropriate procedures regarding any action taken at a meeting in relation to clergy employment. Most courts look to neutral principles such as church documents, legal documents, and/or corporation laws to determine procedural or other rights relevant to the case. Many combine the neutral principles approach with discussion of the nature of the religious institution; that is, is it hierarchical or congregational? With the exception of cases where the clergy member has a written contract for a term of years entitling the clergy member to specific pay regardless of the basis for termination, the most that a clergy member can expect from a civil court is an order finding that the church failed to follow its own procedures and thus the action taken is void, and the clergy member is entitled to any lost compensation or clergy status that occurred as the result of the procedurally flawed decision. Of course, there is then nothing to stop a church or church faction from using proper procedures to achieve the same ends. The clergy member may continue with the church if the faction seeking his or her ouster cannot prevail under proper procedures (which is sometimes the reason those procedures were not followed), but courts will not question substantive decisions made by a church using proper church procedures.

In congregational churches, unless the church constitution or bylaws provide otherwise, the procedure is generally a majority vote of the congregation at a properly called meeting that provides adequate notice to congregants and clergy. Courts defer completely to such decisions when made according to church procedures. In hierarchical churches, the procedures generally are laid out in church documents, and courts give total deference to substantive decisions made by proper church authorities in conformity with church procedures. Some courts have an almost per se rule of never hearing clergy employment disputes even when procedural irregularities exist, as long as written and binding contract rights are not involved. Even when contract rights are involved, most courts will

138 ADVANCED INTRODUCTION TO LAW AND RELIGION

not determine whether a termination or discipline of a clergy member violated the contract, because it is up to church officials to determine the substantive questions regarding just cause and similar employment concepts. Courts will enforce clear contract rights but will not question church decisions arrived at by following church procedures.

Some seemingly nonclergy employees, such as choir directors, are governed by the same doctrine as clergy in most jurisdictions. As explained in *Hossana-Tabor* and *Morrissey-Bereu*, the religious entity has broad power in determining what employees count as clergy for ministerial exception purposes and there is a constitutional duty for courts to defer to the religious entity since the *Hossana-Tabor* and *Morrissey-Bereu* cases were decided. Yet many religious institutions have employees recognized as nonclergy employees to whom the ministerial exception does not apply. Examples would include secretarial and custodial staff (assuming the entity does not consider them "ministers"), who are not necessarily central to the religious aspects of the church. Most courts that address employment cases involving this type of employee will use contract language and general employment law concepts (to the extent that churches are not immune from those laws) to determine outcomes.

In some other systems courts and other civil authorities follow a similar approach, where they leave hiring decisions to the religious organization, but there are a good number of systems that still require religious entities to follow antidiscrimination laws at the very least. These latter systems often make exceptions for religious discrimination so that a religion can have a requirement that its clergy and teachers of the faith be from the same religion. Some of these systems may also have exceptions for gender or sexual orientation discrimination, but not all do.

At the other end of the spectrum are systems where governments must approve the appointment of clergy or even appoint the clergy themselves. This has led to disputes in several situations. For example, in the *Case of Serif v Greece*,[9] government authorities arrested and convicted a Muslim clergy member who had been made Mufti by the religious community, who voluntarily followed him, for fulfilling that role even though the government had appointed someone else as Mufti. The ECHR found that the prosecution and conviction violated Article 9 of the European

---

[9]   ECHR, March 14, 2000.

Convention on Human Rights and that the prosecution defied the importance of "religious pluralism in a democratic society."

In fact, the ECHR has decided several cases involving religious employment. Given the large number of systems that exist within the ECHR's jurisdiction, there is no one rule that would work for all the legal systems. A few general principles can be gleaned from these cases as a whole. First, religious entities are entitled to a good bit of deference in hiring and retention decisions for clergy and teachers under Article 9. Second, employees also have rights that may need to be balanced against the rights of the religious entity. Thus, complete deference to religious entities in hiring or retention decisions involving clergy or teachers of the faith could violate the Convention in some circumstances. Third, when nation states involve themselves in hiring or retention decisions for clergy or teachers of the faith, they need to respect the notion of religious pluralism, which allows religions and their clergy to not be pigeonholed by the state into one religious model. This will sometimes limit the nation state's ability to make hiring and retention decisions for clergy and teachers of the faith, as was seen in the *Serif v Greece* case mentioned above. Related to all of the above, religious autonomy and authority are important for religious entities, and these concepts, along with the principles of neutrality and proportionality when state action is involved, are important under the Convention.

6.4   Liability of religious entities for employee conduct, including clergy abuse

An issue that has long existed, but which has finally come to greater legal and public attention, is abuse by clergy. It is important to note at the outset that clergy abuse is just one subset of situations where those who hold forms of power over vulnerable people abuse that power. Most clergy would never engage in this type of conduct, but even a small subset of clergy who engage in abuse can inflict massive harm on their victims and society as a whole. Clergy abuse, however, raises an issue that does not arise in other abuse situations, namely: What role does the doctrine of religious autonomy play in addressing clergy abuse? In almost every system in the world the individual clergy member can be prosecuted and sued, but what happens when a religious entity knows of the conduct and does nothing—or, worse, places that clergy member in a position where the clergy member can continue to abuse victims? What role should a religious system's views on forgiveness and repentance play in this calculus?

In the US, as in many other systems, courts have held explicitly that sexual and/or physical abuse is not part of the duties of clergy members or church employees and therefore finding these individuals liable for their conduct would not raise religious questions. To the extent that physical assault or threats are argued to be part of a religious tradition, courts tend to find that the state's interest in protecting individuals from assault and battery outweighs any free exercise or autonomy right asserted.

Claims against a religious entity for negligent hiring, supervision, and retention raise several issues. These claims arise in a variety of circumstances. One of the most common is abuse of congregants or their family members by clergy. Other claims can involve failure to adequately supervise employees under circumstances where injury is reasonably foreseeable. The latter claims generally involve garden-variety negligence, so raise fewer issues than claims related to abuse or other intentional behavior. For example, failure to adequately supervise staff at a camp or religious school program, thus leading to injury, could generally be addressed under normal negligence principles without raising serious ecclesiastical questions.

Conversely, claims that often arise in the abuse context, such as negligent hiring or retention of clergy or other church employees with a religious role, such as religious schoolteachers, can raise significant ecclesiastical concerns. The same could be said for claims of negligent supervision of these types of employees. Still, a majority of US courts recognize negligent supervision claims while rejecting negligent hiring and retention claims in the clergy abuse context. Of course, some courts recognize the latter claims while others do not recognize even negligent supervision claims.

The key is that claims based on negligent employment of clergy and other employees with religious roles can raise important ecclesiastical concerns. These concerns include the right of religious entities to determine qualifications for a position based on religious principles and/or traditions, the role of religious requirements in disciplining employees, the role of forgiveness and belief in rehabilitation rather than dismissal, the role that church hierarchy plays in determining the need for and structure of supervisory relationships, internal codes of discipline, and the lack of a church hierarchy to supervise clergy in some congregational settings. Courts are often concerned about getting involved in these situations because of the likelihood of having to address ecclesiastical questions. Some courts point out that these sorts of claims could be characterized as claims for clergy malpractice, which US courts do not recognize.

Yet in many cases courts are willing to address clergy abuse issues, because negligence can be determined without any need to address ecclesiastical concerns. For example, consider a case where a clergy member in a hierarchical church is involved in sexually abusing children. The relevant church hierarchy is aware of the behavior and, rather than remove the clergy member from contact with children, the church transfers him to another church, where he abuses other children. The church hierarchy never warns anyone at the new church of the past conduct. When the victims of abuse at the new church sue, the church hierarchy claims they could not terminate the clergy member due to faith in rehabilitation and forgiveness. A court could not address the credibility or value of the church's defense, but courts have held that under these circumstances the church was negligent in supervising the clergy member even if the defense is taken as true, because it should not have allowed the clergy member to have further contact with children under the circumstances, or that any such contact should have been carefully supervised, and/or the relevant hierarchical church officials should have warned the members or board of the new church.

This raises the key issue in negligent supervision, hiring, and retention claims. It is key that these are not claims for vicarious liability. The religious entity is liable for its own conduct or failure to act. Vicarious liability for a clergy member's conduct could raise a number of religious issues. Even without these additional ecclesiastical issues it would be hard to prevail on a vicarious liability claim, because employers are rarely vicariously liable for intentional torts committed by employees, and it would be nearly impossible to demonstrate that sexual abuse is within the scope of a clergy member's employment. Thus, it is important to remain focused on the fact that claims for negligent supervision, hiring, and retention are based on the religious entity's own conduct *vis-à-vis* the offending clergy member and victims.

This explains why claims for negligent hiring and retention are often frowned upon but claims for negligent supervision are more successful.

The former claims may require civil courts to address the religiously charged issues that religious entities engage in when making decisions about clergy hiring and retention. Negligent supervision claims are often focused on the religious entity's failure to adequately supervise those who it hires or retains when that entity has reason to believe congregants or others are being harmed by those individuals. Knowledge of the harmful conduct or its likelihood can be central to these cases. In some cases, courts require actual knowledge of past abusive conduct by the relevant clergy member or employee, or at the very least knowledge of current inappropriate behavior. Other courts have applied constructive knowledge in circumstances where it would be unreasonable for the entity not to have known of the risk of harm.

Where religious entities knowingly place an employee who has engaged in sexual or other physical abuse in a situation where that employee will have contact with those similarly situated to the employee's past victims, courts are even more likely to find liability when the abuse happens again. Under these circumstances the court may find or presume a failure to adequately supervise because the clergy member or employee was able to abuse again. A few courts do not recognize these claims even under the worst circumstances out of concern that they would have to determine ecclesiastical questions to decide the case.

Another common basis for successful abuse claims arises when a religious entity threatens the victim or the victim's family with retaliation if the abuse claims are made public, tries to minimize harm to itself through counseling, or tries to manipulate the victim or the victim's family through other mechanisms. Here it is the entity's intentional or reckless conduct that gives rise to liability, rather than failure to supervise an employee or clergy member.

Moreover, there are several state statutes that specifically hold entities liable when they fail to adequately supervise an employee and/or negligently hire or retain an employee, resulting in abuse. Some of these statutes have provisions that specifically apply to religious organizations. Still others extend the statute of limitations for abuse claims where the religious (or other) entity's own conduct inhibited or prevented timelier claims.

Claims for negligent counseling or negligent ministering also arise on occasion. These claims are rarely successful because such claims either are directly based in clergy malpractice or closely resemble clergy malpractice. As noted above, claims for clergy malpractice are virtually never successful.

There are, however, a few cases where claims for negligent counseling by a religious entity have been recognized. These cases usually involve situations where the counselor held themselves out as engaging in secular counseling, or where the counselor's secular credentials were touted, or where these credentials were touted but did not exist. In a few cases, claims were successful where the religious counselor knew or should have known that the patient needed secular help and discouraged that help or failed to suggest that help. More often than not, however, claims for failure to refer to secular counselors are unsuccessful because those claims raise ecclesiastical questions.

Finally, as noted above, vicarious liability may be available against religious entities for regular sorts of negligence by employees, such as an employee driving a church vehicle negligently. Importantly, however, in cases where clergy or other church employees abuse congregants or others, the clergy member or employee is almost always found to be acting outside of the scope of employment. As explained above, the best way to find a religious entity liable for harm resulting from physical, mental, or sexual abuse is through a claim for negligent supervision or other claim that focuses on the religious entity's conduct.

Significantly, vicarious liability does not generally apply to intentional torts in the US and most of the conduct in abuse cases falls within intentional torts. There are, however, a few exceptions to this general rule. The exceptions usually arise where a religious entity has been found to ratify the intentional conduct (and, of course, the entity can be liable for its own intentional conduct).

In many other nations all or most forms of clergy abuse are, as in the US, crimes, so much of the debate centers on civil liability. In most systems the clergy member will be held liable for any abuse, but whether the religious entity itself can be held liable may differ vastly between systems. In some systems religious entities have absolute immunity from civil lawsuits or violations. In other systems religious entities are treated no differently from other entities when sued for negligent hiring, retention or supervision, or for vicarious liability. In still other systems, much like in many states in the US, the liability of religious entities for clergy abuse is fact-sensitive and may involve questions of church autonomy or the ecclesiastical abstention concept. The above discussion of the US system captures most, but not all, of the issues that arise in these latter systems.

7. Conclusion

Hopefully this book has given you some added insight into the many issues that arise in the law and religion context. The field of law and religion is a hard one to summarize even in an advanced introduction designed for those who already have some background in the area. In addition to the many issues that can arise—and this book covered many but not all of them—there are an array of legal systems in which law and religion issues are evaluated. These systems run the gamut from highly secular to theocratic.[1] This book focused heavily on the US because of the incredible amount of litigation and law involving law and religion in the US, but other systems such as the European Convention on Human Rights, the Japanese system, the French system, the Canadian system, and the Singaporean system were all addressed in places. The idea is not to provide you with a discussion of every system in the world—an approach far beyond the scope of this advanced introduction—but to provide you with examples that are reflected in many systems around the world.

After a brief introduction, the book began with a conceptual introduction to the principles that often undergird law and religion issues, such as liberty, equality, neutrality, separation, accommodation, nonpreferential-ism, and tradition. These underlying concepts are sometimes expressly used by courts or legislators and sometimes implicit in how legal systems address law and religion questions. From there, the book addressed a variety of questions involving religious freedom. Some of these have come to the fore more in recent years and some have been discussed and debated for centuries. The topic then moved to questions about government support for or promotion of religion, often referred to as establishment of religion questions as per the US terminology. Finally, the book addressed questions of religious autonomy such as the resolution of

---

[1] As was explained in the introduction theocracies are beyond the scope of this book.

intrareligious disputes, employment decisions by religious entities, and liability for clergy abuse.

As a practical matter, each of these chapters, and in fact many of the subsections within each chapter, could occupy a book(s). The goal was to give the reader, as the title of this book suggests, an advanced introduction to the many concepts, rules, and questions that arise in law and religion. The book is obviously not comprehensive but hopefully it enabled you to gain a more in-depth understanding of the issues addressed herein.

Finally, this book breaks down the main issues within law and religion into separate chapters and sections. This does not mean, however, that these issues easily fit into any one category. Many of these issues overlap and interconnect in complex ways. The book was able to address some of those overlaps and interconnections, but it remains essential to understand that the topics within are based on substantive and organizational concerns and the chapter and section breakdowns should not be viewed as barriers between the chapters and sections but rather as signposts along the fascinating path of a deeper understanding of law and religion.

Index

accommodation 11, 15–16, 27, 30, 44, 52–3
adoption 29, 31, 35, 38
American Humanist 87
animal rights 30, 36–7
Arkansas 61–2
Australia 61
Austria 46
authoritarian regimes 1

Balanced Treatment for Creation-Science and Evolution in Public School Instruction Act (1981) 62–3
Belgium 36–8
bias 7–8
birth control 40–42
Boudreaux, Edward 64
Brennan, Justice 83
Breyer, Justice 86, 88, 90
Buddhism 35, 104
Burger, Justice 80

Calabrese, Judge 104
Canada 52, 54
ceremonial deism 105
Chabad-Lubavich 82
Chanukah 82–3
charities 35, 52, 112–13, 115–16, 119–20, 123
China 1
Christianity
    Catholic church 29, 31, 35, 49, 82
    Christmas 80–82
    churches 5–6, 115, 119–21, 126–33

creationism 64
crucifixes 72–3
ECHR and 71
France 7
King James bible 83
legislative prayer 6
nativity scenes 80–81, 83
Protestants 35
social conservatives (US) 16
Civil War (US) 126
clergy
    abuse by 139–44
    funding 47
    hiring supervision and retention of 135–9
Cleveland, Ohio 108
conceptual foundations 4–23
    accommodation 15–16
    defining religion 18–23
    equality 5–9
    liberty 9–11
    neutrality 11–13
    nonpreferentialism 17
    separationism 13–15
    tradition 17–18
Confederacy 126
Confucianism 19, 97
conscientious objectors 20–22
COVID-19 5–7, 31, 40, 42–3, 49–52
creationism 55–69

Declaration of Independence (US) 83, 84, 85–6
discrimination 45–53
    adoption 31
    Buddhist attitudes to 35

147

148 ADVANCED INTRODUCTION TO LAW AND RELIGION

by religion 51–3
COVID-19 5–7
definitions and 20
ECHR cases 45–6
employment 3, 45
exceptions for religious entities 138
France 7
Free Exercise Clause and 108
general applicability laws and 27
Japan 35
law and 27
LGBT 34
prayer case 6–7
United States 5–7, 12, 46–53
what counts as 5–6, 12
disparate impact 8
District of Columbia 87

ecclesiastical abstention concept 125, 144
ecclesiastical questions 120, 125–35, 140–44
equal access 15, 55, 78, 91, 94
equality 5–9
Establishment Clause *see* United States: Constitution; Establishment Clause
Europe
    diversity within 14
    Eastern Europe 72, 112
    exemption situations 15–16, 43
    public property and religious entities 94
    recognized and unrecognized religions 92
    religious symbolism in schools 69–77
    Western Europe 30
European Charter of Fundamental Rights 37
European Convention on Human Rights 3, 4, 70–71, 73, 75, 138–9
European Court of Human Rights (ECHR)
    accommodation 16
    Article 2 of Protocol 1 71, 76
    Article 8 74

Article 9 36–9, 45, 71–7, 139
Article 10 74
Article 14 36, 38
cases decided
    Dahlab v Switzerland 73–4
    Dogru v France 75, 76
    Kervanci v France 75, 76
    Köse and 93 others v Turkey 75–6
    Kurtulmus v Turkey 74
    Lautsi and Others v Italy 71–4, 77
    Leyla Sahin v Turkey 75
    Religionsgemeinschaft der Zeugen Jehovas and Others v Austria 45
    Savez crkava "Riječ života and Others v Croatia 45
    Serif v Greece 138–9
    Singh v France 75, 76
EU and 38
freedom of religion and for-profit entities 39
jurisdiction 3–4
limitations on religious freedom 52
minority religions 73, 77
neutrality 12, 13
public safety laws 52
religious employment cases 139
religious symbolism in schools 70–77
slaughter laws 36–7
European Court of Justice (ECJ) 3–4, 36–8, 52
European Union (EU) 3
    animal welfare principles 37
    ECHR and 38
    government and religion 55
    national laws 3
    neutrality 5
    religious freedom 4
    school prayers 56
evolution 61–7, 69
exemptions 27–45
    accommodation and 15–16
    adoption 31

INDEX   149

conflicting with rights of other
    39–45
demarcation between religion and
    non-religion 28–9
disparate impact and 8–9
ECHR 36–9
Free Exercise Clause 10
general applicability laws 27–8
Japan 32–6
LGBT 34–5, 44
pandemics 32, 35–6
slaughter laws 30–31, 33–4
United States 29–32
US and Japan 33–4

Finding Darwin's God (Kenneth
    Miller) 65
Flemish 38
for-profit entities 24, 26–7, 39–44
fostering 31
    see also adoption
France
    Christianity 7
    ECHR cases 76–7
    government and religion 54, 55
    government funding for 106–7
    Islam 7
    Japan and 97
    Judaism 7
    laïcité 7, 14, 106
    nonpreferentialism 17
    separationism 14–15
Fraternal Order of Eagles 87
Free Exercise Clause *see* United States:
    Constitution: Free Exercise
    Clause
free speech 41, 59–60, 63, 91–4,
    99–100
freedom (of religion)
    a broad term 24
    conflicting rights 39–45
    definitions 19, 20, 22
    ECHR and Canada 52
    for-profit entities 26
    Free Exercise Clause 53
    individuals 25
    Japan 32, 35
    United States 4, 26, 28

funding 106–123
    clergy 47
    tax credits 110
    tax exemptions 111–23
        Singapore 123
        United States 111–22
            churches, defining 115,
                119–21
            Parsonage Exemption
                121–2
            political activity and
                lobbying 115–16
            private inurement
                112–16

general applicable laws 10, 16, 27–8
Germany 17, 38, 97, 107
gerrymandering 46, 104, 108
Ginsburg, Justice 41, 89
God 20, 63, 65–7, 83, 105

halal butchers 29, 30, 33–4, 36–7
Hasidim 82
headscarves 73–4
hijabs 75–6
Holy Name Society 82
Hungary 72

"In God We Trust" 105
intelligent design 61, 63–9
intrareligious disputes 124–35
    government involvement in
        124–5
    Japan 134–5
    United States 125–34
        church property disputes
            126–33
        congregational disputes
            128–30
        express and implied
            trusts 128
        hierarchical churches
            130
        Watson v Jones ruling
            127
        schisms 133–4
        state incorporation laws 133

terminology 125
Iran 1
Islam 7, 29, 30, 36–8, 71–2, 138
Italy 72

Japan
    Act on National Flag and Anthem
        Law (1999) 56–7
    Constitution
        Article 12 35
        Article 20
            accommodationist
                approach 16
            for-profit entities 40
            funding 107
            paragraph 3 19, 96
            religion and
                government 4
            right to religious
                freedom 32
            Sunagawa shrine case
                95, 97
        Article 89 4, 95–6, 97, 107
        full protection for all
            religions 92
        national anthem 56
    creationism of no interest in 61
    Cultural Heritage Sites 94, 98–9
    exemption situations 16, 32–6
    government and religion 54, 55
    government funding for 107
    intrareligious disputes 134–5
    Kimigayo 56
    LGBTQ 34
    Ministry of Education, Culture,
        Sports, Science and
        Technology (MEXT) 107
    neutrality 5
    public property and religious
        entities 94–9
    public welfare considerations 35
    Religious Juridical Persons Act
        (Shuukyou Houjin Hou) 4,
        34, 40, 92, 134–5
    same-sex marriages 34–5
    school prayers 56–7
    separation of politics and religion
        13–14

Shinto 14, 33, 95–7
Sunagawa 95–6
Supreme Court decisions 19, 32–3
    Kobe Technical College 33
    refusal to sing national
        anthem 56–7
    similarities to European
        systems 97
    Sunagawa Sorachibuto
        Shrine Case 95–6, 97
    Ujiko 95–6
Jehovah's Witnesses 1, 25, 32, 45, 70
Jewish War Veterans' Association 89
Judaism 7, 29, 30, 36–8, 71–2

Keith, Bill 62, 63, 64
King James bible 83
Kitzmiller v Dover Area School District
    66, 67, 68
kosher butchers 29, 30, 33–4, 36–7

Laycock, Douglas 12
legislative prayer 6–7, 17–18, 54–5, 87,
    103–5
LGBTQ 29, 34–5, 44, 52
liberty 5, 9–11, 82
Little Rock, Arkansas 61
Louisiana 62–3, 64

Maastricht, Treaty of 4
Maine 49–50, 111
menorahs 82–3
Miller, Kenneth 65
Missouri 48
moment of silence laws 77
Montana 110
monuments 18
Myanmar 1

nativity scenes 80–81
naturalism 65
Nebraska 104
neutrality
    Arkansas case 62
    central principle 5
    examples of neutral principles
        132–3

INDEX 151

importance of 86, 139
Köse case 76
Lemon case 84
Trinity Lutheran case 109
New York 6, 42–3, 50–51
nonpreferentialism 5, 17
North Korea 1

O'Connor, Justice 81–2, 86
Okinawa 19, 97, 98
Osaka 34

pandemics 5, 29, 32, 35, 39, 43, 51
Parsonage Exemption 112, 121–2
Poland 72
preferential treatment 8
Presbyterian Church 126–7
private inurement 112–16
public property 78–105
    access to by religious groups 91–4
    ceremonial deism 105
    change in status of land 98–9
    free speech issues 99–103
    grants of public property to
        religious groups 94–9
    legislative prayer 103–5
    religious symbols on 78–91
    US categories of 92–3

Rehnquist, Justice (US Supreme
    Court) 17, 80, 86
religion
    Buddhism 35, 104
    Christianity *see* Christianity
    Confucianism 19, 97
    defining 18–23
        no clear demarcation 18–19,
            20, 23, 28–9
        United States on 20
    discrimination *see* discrimination
    exemptions for 8–9, 10, 15–16,
        27–45
    faith based 10
    for-profit entities 24, 26–7
    historical sites 97
    Islam 7, 29, 30, 36–8, 71, 138
    Judaism 7, 29, 30, 36–8, 71

legislative prayer 17–18, 103–5
    practice oriented 10
    recognised and unrecognised 20,
        54, 91–2
    religious entities 25–6
    Shinto 14, 33, 95–7
    supernatural element 23
religious autonomy 124–44
    clergy 135–44
    intrareligious disputes 124–35
religious symbols 69–77, 78–91
    Christmas 80–82
    legal tests problematic 79
    nativity scenes 80–81, 83
    "passive symbols" 72–3
    Ten Commandments 70, 80, 83–7
Rohingya 1
Russia 1, 70

same-sex marriages 26, 34–5, 38
San Francisco 30
Santeria 46, 109
Sapporo 34
Saudi Arabia 1
schisms 124–6, 133–4
schools (France) 14–15, 17
    see also United States: schools
secular purpose test 84
secularism 7, 8, 14, 15, 17, 72
separationism 13–15
    American success with 86
    Establishment Clause, purpose
        of 88
    Japan 56–7, 92
    neutrality and 12
    strict separation 14
    United States, separationism
        a hollow shell 55
    various countries 54–5
Singapore 111, 123
slaughter laws 29, 30–31, 33–4, 36–8,
    47
slavery 126
Smith, Steven 11
Souter, Justice 84–5
South Africa 16
state incorporation laws 133, 137
substantive neutrality 12–13

152 ADVANCED INTRODUCTION TO LAW AND RELIGION

Sullivan, Winnifred Fallers 28
Supreme Court (Japan) *see* Japan:
    Supreme Court
Supreme Court (US)
    accommodation 16
    cases decided
        Abington Township v
            Schempp 57, 58
        ACLU v McCreary County
            83, 86, 87, 88, 90–91,
            103
        American Legion v American
            Humanist 89, 90
        Burwell v Hobby Lobby 26,
            40–42, 52
        Carson v Makin 49, 111
        Church of the Lukumi Babalu
            Aye v City of Hialeah
            46–7, 49, 108–9
        Citizens United v Federal
            Election Commission
            41
        County of Allegheny v
            American Civil
            Liberties Union 82
        Davis v Beason 20, 22
        Edwards v Aguillard 63–5, 67
        Engel v Vitale 57, 58
        Epperson v Arkansas 61–2, 65
        Espinoza v Montana Dept.
            of Revenue 48, 49, 50,
            110–111
        Fulton v City of Philadelphia
            28, 31
        Hosanna-Tabor Evangelical
            Lutheran Church v
            Equal Employment
            Opportunity
            Commission 136, 138
        Jones v Wolf 132
        Kennedy v Bremerton School
            District 58, 60–61, 69,
            79, 90–91, 99–103
        Lemon v Kurtmann 58–60
            ACLU v McCreary
                 County and 83
            calls for rejection 90

        Kennedy v Bremerton
            School District
            overturns 99, 102
        Kitzmiller case and 68
        legislative prayer and
            104
        plurality opinion and 87
        purpose of lemon test
            and 84
        Locke v Davey 47
        Lynch v Donnelly 80–82, 83,
            87, 90
        Marsh v Chambers 87, 104–5
        Maryland and Virginia
            Eldership of the
            Churches of God v
            Church of God at
            Sharpsburg, Inc.
            131–2
        Masterpiece Cakeshop v
            Colorado Civil Rights
            Commission 26, 44,
            51, 52
        Our Lady of Guadalupe
            School v
            Morrissey-Berru 136,
            138
        Presbyterian Church in U.S.
            v Mary Elizabeth
            Blue Hull Memorial
            Presbyterian Church
            131, 132
        Regan v Taxation with
            Representation 118
        Roman Catholic Diocese of
            Brooklyn v Cuomo 5,
            6, 36, 42–3, 50
        Santa Fe Indep. School
            District v Doe 59, 102,
            103
        South Bay United Pentecostal
            Church v Newsom 5,
            6, 43
        Stone v Graham 70, 84–5, 87
        Town of Greece v Galloway
            104–105
        Trinity Lutheran v Comer 48,
            49, 50, 109–111

United States v Ballard 22
United States v Seeger 20–1, 22
Van Orden v Perry 80, 86, 88, 90
Watson v Jones 126–32
Welsh v United States 21–2
Zelman v Simmons-Harris 49, 108
Covid-19 5, 31
discrimination 45
general applicability laws 27
Georgia Supreme Court 131
legislative prayer 6
make-up of 17
Montana Supreme Court 110
non-discrimination doctrine 46
separationism 12, 15, 55
"special disabilities" 48
uncertainty on future direction 55, 58
Switzerland 73
systemic bias 7–8

Ten Commandments 70, 80, 83–7
Texas 86, 87
theocracies 1
Tillich, Paul 80
Tokyo 34
tradition 17–18, 86–90
ceremonial deism 105
Christianity 16
churches and congregations 120
locker room prayers 101
nativity scenes 80–81
property disputes 131–2
Treen, David C. 62
Turkey 74–5
Turkmenistan 1

United Kingdom 38, 54, 56
United States (US)
accommodation 16
Affordable Care Act 40
Age Discrimination in Employment Act 136
Americans with Disabilities Act 136

birth control 40–42
ceremonial deism 105
churches 5–6
clergy 135–8
congregational churches 137–8
ministerial exception 135
conscientious objectors 20–22
Constitution
Establishment Clause (First Amendment)
County of Allegheny case 82
core principles 86
creationism and 55–61, 67, 68
defining religion and 19
dual nature of 87
ecclesiastical cases 130
funding the clergy 47
government and private religious speech 100
government funding under 107–9
Justice Breyer on 88
Kennedy v Bremerton School District 102–3
legislative prayer case 6
ministerial exception 135
Parsonage Exemption 122
religious groups access to public forums 93–4
separationism 13
separationism and neutrality 12
Ten Commandments plaques 70
tradition and 17
war memorial case 89
Free Exercise Clause
accommodation 15
adoption 31

anti-discrimination
principles
changed 50–51
COVID-19 cases 6, 50
ecclesiastical churches
130
*Espinoza v Montana
Dept. of Revenue*
48
general applicability
cases 10
government funding
and 108–111
interpreting
discrimination
108
Locke v Davey 47
ministerial exception
135
neutrality and
discrimination
12
religious exemptions
under 43, 53
Santeria case 46–7
*Trinity Lutheran v
Comer* 48
Free Speech Clause 59, 60,
93–4, 100
important role of 3
not the only arbiter 4
defining religion 20
Equal Employment Opportunity
Commission 3
Federal Internal Revenue Code
(IRS Code) 3, 112, 119, 121
for-profit entities 24, 26–7, 40–41
free speech 99–103
"In God We Trust" 105
Internal Revenue Service (IRS) 3,
113, 115, 117–20
intrareligious disputes 125–34
legislative prayer 103–5
litigation, pervasiveness of 2
neutrality 5
no concept of a "recognised
religion" 92
nonpreferentialism 17

public property 78–94, 99–105
access to property by
religious groups 91–4
categories of 92–3
ceremonial deism 105
free speech issues 99–103
legislative prayer 103–5
religious symbols 78–91
public schools 55–6, 57–69
creationism/intelligent
design 61–9
moment of silence laws 77
prayer 55–6, 57–61
religious exemptions *see*
exemptions
Religious Freedom Restoration
Act (RFRA)
accommodational approach
16
exemptions required by 29
federal law 30
for-profit entities 26
importance of 3, 4
religious exemptions under
40, 42, 43
state level 44
Religious Land Use and
Institutionalized Persons
Act (RLUIPA) 29
same-sex marriages 26
schools
case studies 79, 87
creationism 61–9
extracurricular access 93
funding 106–8
prayers 55–61, 99
private schools 110, 111
religious schools 110–111,
120, 136, 140
religious symbolism 69–77
sports 101–3
vouchers 49–50, 108, 111
separationism 13–14, 15, 55
state constitutions 3, 4
strict scrutiny 46–7, 48
Supreme Court *see* Supreme
Court
tax system 110–12, 114–16, 118

tradition 17
Treasury, Department of the 117, 122
Universal Military Training and Service Act 20
Vietnam War 20

war memorials 89–90
Washington state 47
wedding vendors 26, 39, 43, 52
Wisconsin 122
World War I 89–90

Titles in the **Elgar Advanced Introductions** series include:

International Political Economy
Benjamin J. Cohen

The Austrian School of Economics
Randall G. Holcombe

Cultural Economics
Ruth Towse

Law and Development
Michael J. Trebilcock and Mariana Mota Prado

International Humanitarian Law
Robert Kolb

International Trade Law
Michael J. Trebilcock

Post Keynesian Economics
J.E. King

International Intellectual Property
Susy Frankel and Daniel J. Gervais

Public Management and Administration
Christopher Pollitt

Organised Crime
Leslie Holmes

Nationalism
Liah Greenfeld

Social Policy
Daniel Béland and Rianne Mahon

Globalisation
Jonathan Michie

Entrepreneurial Finance
Hans Landström

International Conflict and Security Law
Nigel D. White

Comparative Constitutional Law
Mark Tushnet

International Human Rights Law
Dinah L. Shelton

Entrepreneurship
Robert D. Hisrich

International Tax Law
Reuven S. Avi-Yonah

Public Policy
B. Guy Peters

The Law of International Organizations
Jan Klabbers

International Environmental Law
Ellen Hey

International Sales Law
Clayton P. Gillette

Corporate Venturing
Robert D. Hisrich

Public Choice
Randall G. Holcombe

Private Law
Jan M. Smits

Consumer Behavior Analysis
Gordon Foxall

Behavioral Economics
John F. Tomer

Cost–Benefit Analysis
Robert J. Brent

Environmental Impact Assessment
Angus Morrison-Saunders

Comparative Constitutional Law,
Second Edition
Mark Tushnet

National Innovation Systems
Cristina Chaminade, Bengt-Åke Lundvall and Shagufta Haneef

Ecological Economics
Matthias Ruth

Private International Law and Procedure
Peter Hay

Freedom of Expression
Mark Tushnet

Law and Globalisation
Jaakko Husa

Regional Innovation Systems
Bjørn T. Asheim, Arne Isaksen and Michaela Trippl

International Political Economy
Second Edition
Benjamin J. Cohen

International Tax Law
Second Edition
Reuven S. Avi-Yonah

Social Innovation
Frank Moulaert and Diana MacCallum

The Creative City
Charles Landry

International Trade Law
Michael J. Trebilcock and Joel Trachtman

European Union Law
Jacques Ziller

Planning Theory
Robert A. Beauregard

Tourism Destination Management
Chris Ryan

International Investment Law
August Reinisch

Sustainable Tourism
David Weaver

Austrian School of Economics
Second Edition
Randall G. Holcombe

U.S. Criminal Procedure
Christopher Slobogin

Platform Economics
Robin Mansell and W. Edward Steinmueller

Public Finance
Vito Tanzi

Feminist Economics
Joyce P. Jacobsen

Human Dignity and Law
James R. May and Erin Daly

Space Law
Frans G. von der Dunk

National Accounting
John M. Hartwick

Legal Research Methods
Ernst Hirsch Ballin

Privacy Law
Megan Richardson

International Human Rights Law
Second Edition
Dinah L. Shelton

Law and Artificial Intelligence
Woodrow Barfield and Ugo Pagallo

Politics of International Human
Rights
David P. Forsythe

Community-based Conservation
Fikret Berkes

Global Production Networks
Neil M. Coe

Mental Health Law
Michael L. Perlin

Law and Literature
Peter Goodrich

Creative Industries
John Hartley

Global Administration Law
Sabino Cassese

Housing Studies
William A.V. Clark

Global Sports Law
Stephen F. Ross

Public Policy
B. Guy Peters

Empirical Legal Research
Herbert M. Kritzer

Cities
Peter J. Taylor

Law and Entrepreneurship
Shubha Ghosh

Mobilities
Mimi Sheller

Technology Policy
*Albert N. Link and James
Cunningham*

Urban Transport Planning
Kevin J. Krizek and David A. King

Legal Reasoning
*Larry Alexander and Emily
Sherwin*

Sustainable Competitive
Advantage in Sales
Lawrence B. Chonko

Law and Development
Second Edition
*Mariana Mota Prado and Michael
J. Trebilcock*

Law and Renewable Energy
Joel B. Eisen

Experience Economy
Jon Sundbo

Marxism and Human Geography
Kevin R. Cox

Maritime Law
Paul Todd

American Foreign Policy
Loch K. Johnson

Water Politics
Ken Conca

Business Ethics
John Hooker

Employee Engagement
Alan M. Saks and Jamie A. Gruman

Governance
Jon Pierre and B. Guy Peters

Demography
Wolfgang Lutz

Environmental Compliance and Enforcement
LeRoy C. Paddock

Migration Studies
Ronald Skeldon

Landmark Criminal Cases
George P. Fletcher

Comparative Legal Methods
Pier Giuseppe Monateri

U.S. Environmental Law
E. Donald Elliott and Daniel C. Esty

Gentrification
Chris Hamnett

Family Policy
Chiara Saraceno

Law and Psychology
Tom R. Tyler

Advertising
Patrick De Pelsmacker

New Institutional Economics
Claude Ménard and Mary M. Shirley

The Sociology of Sport
Eric Anderson and Rory Magrath

The Sociology of Peace Processes
John D. Brewer

Social Protection
James Midgley

Corporate Finance
James A. Brickley and Clifford W. Smith Jr

U.S. Federal Securities Law
Thomas Lee Hazen

Cybersecurity Law
David P. Fidler

The Sociology of Work
Amy S. Wharton

Marketing Strategy
George S. Day

Scenario Planning
Paul Schoemaker

Financial Inclusion
Robert Lensink, Calumn Hamilton and Charles Adjasi

Children's Rights
Wouter Vandenhole and Gamze Erdem Türkelli

Sustainable Careers
Jeffrey H. Greenhaus and Gerard A. Callanan

Business and Human Rights
Peter T. Muchlinski

Spatial Statistics
Daniel A. Griffith and Bin Li

The Sociology of the Self
Shanyang Zhao

Artificial Intelligence in
Healthcare
*Tom Davenport, John Glaser and
Elizabeth Gardner*

Central Banks and Monetary
Policy
*Jakob de Haan and Christiaan
Pattipeilohy*

Megaprojects
*Nathalie Drouin and Rodney
Turner*

Social Capital
Karen S. Cook

Elections and Voting
Ian McAllister

Negotiation
*Leigh Thompson and Cynthia S.
Wang*

Youth Studies
*Howard Williamson and James E.
Côté*

Private Equity
*Paul A. Gompers and Steven N.
Kaplan*

Digital Marketing
Utpal Dholakia

Water Economics and Policy
Ariel Dinar

Disaster Risk Reduction

Douglas Paton

Social Movements and Political
Protests
Karl-Dieter Opp

Radical Innovation
Joe Tidd

Pricing Strategy and Analytics
Vithala R. Rao

Bounded Rationality
Clement A. Tisdell

International Food Law
Neal D. Fortin

International Conflict and Security
Law
Second Edition
Nigel D. White

Entrepreneurial Finance
Second Edition
Hans Landström

US Civil Liberties
Susan N. Herman

Resilience
Fikret Berkes

Insurance Law
Robert H. Jerry III

Applied Green Criminology
Rob White

Law and Religion
Frank S. Ravitch

Social Policy
Second Edition
Daniel Béland and Rianne Mahon

Substantive Criminal Law
Stephen J. Morse

Cross-Border Insolvency Law
Reinhard Bork

Behavioral Finance
H. Kent Baker, John R. Nofsinger, and Victor Ricciardi

Critical Global Development
Uma Kothari and Elise Klein

Private International Law and
Procedure
Second Edition
Peter Hay

Victimology
Sandra Walklate

Party Politics
Richard S. Katz

Contract Law and Theory
Brian Bix